# The RAF REGIMENT
## at WAR
### 1942-1946

PER ARDUA

# The RAF REGIMENT at WAR
## 1942-1946

### Kingsley M. Oliver

LEO COOPER

First published in Great Britain in 2002 by
Leo Cooper
an imprint of Pen & Sword Books Limited
47 Church Street, Barnsley, South Yorkshire S70 2AS

Copyright © 2002 by Kingsley M. Oliver

*For up-to date information on other titles
produced under the Pen & Sword imprint,
please telephone or write to:*

Pen & Sword Books Limited
FREEPOST
47 Church Street
Barnsley
South Yorkshire
S70 2BR

Telephone (24 hours): 01226 734555

**ISBN 0-85052-852-6**

A CIP catalogue record of this book is available from the British Library

**Printed by CPI UK**

# Contents

# ACKNOWLEDGEMENTS

As in any study of the events of the Second World War, the background and much of the detail has depended upon the official histories of the various campaigns, as published by Her Majesty's Stationery Office. In addition to other material in the public domain in the Public Record Office, the Imperial War Museum, regimental archives and libraries, my researches have been enhanced by the published works of, among others, Chester Wilmot (*The Struggle for Europe*), Norman Gelb (*Desperate Venture – Operation Torch*), FM Sir Bernard Montgomery (*From Normandy to the Baltic*), FM Sir William Slim (*Defeat into Victory*), Air Commodore Henry Probert (*The Forgotten Air Force*), Norman Franks (*The Battle of the Airfields*) and, of course, Squadron Leader Nicholas Tucker (*In Adversity*) for his definitive record of RAF Regiment honours and awards.

The personal reminiscences of those WWII veterans who have been kind enough to contribute letters, diaries and photographs have been extremely valuable and for similar material belonging to those now sadly deceased but which has been made available by their relatives, is equally appreciated by the author.

Accordingly, my thanks are due to Richard Auld, Ronald Gullen Beales, Charles Beddow, L Bowring, Douglas Burgiss, Norman Buckingham, ML Connolly, Dennis Cook, Roly Cooper (for his father, the late Gp Capt Stan Cooper), Richard Cox, Derrick Dean, Robert Edwards, CAG Eyles, Roland George, Graham Gow, Mark Hobden, Colin Hope, Ron House, Frederick Jeffrey, Maurice Jones, Charles Killeen, Arthur Langham, George Lawrence, Jim Lennon, WT McLellan, Randle Manwaring, A Mercer, Alex Miller, W Mitchell, Norman Parker, Bill Raymond, Len Read, Bernie Reid, DR Rescoe, Ronald Rollitt, Norman Salmon (for his father, the late Colonel Morrey Salmon), Peter Silk (for his father, the late Flt Lt Philip Silk), MJ Slee, Les Smith, J Smith, RT Statham, WD Stewart, Ted Stiles, Eric Westrope, Mike Williams and Frank Winfield.

I am grateful to the Trustees of the Imperial War Museum, Controller of Her Majesty's Stationery Office and the Public Record Office for permission to reproduce photographs from their respective archives, and to Phil May for recapturing the action at Helmond in November 1944.

I am, as always, indebted to Air Vice-Marshal Donald Pocock for his wise counsel – and for kindly writing the preface to this volume. I am grateful to Simon Hadley for his advice on design and for his skill in enabling small, old and often damaged photographs to be transformed into models of clarity. My sincere thanks also go to Squadron Leader Trevor Hadley for the unfailing support and encouragement which he has given in bringing the publication of this work to fruition. Finally, I record my appreciation for all my wife Audrey has done to assist me in this project.

Kingsley Oliver
Bromley, June 2002

# PREFACE

By

Air Vice-Marshal D. A. Pocock CBE
Commandant-General RAF Regiment 1973-75

The loss of Crete to the Germans in 1941 confirmed, beyond all doubt, the vulnerability of our airfields to ground and air attack and the British government reacted with urgency to create a specialist airfield defence corps as an integral part of the Royal Air Force, designated as the "Royal Air Force Regiment", which came into being at the beginning of 1942.

While the new force was being formed in the United Kingdom, officers and airmen already in overseas theatres were reorganized into RAF Regiment units and priority was given to the Middle East where the forward airfields, on which the Desert Air Force depended, were under attack from enemy ground and air forces. The successful conclusion of the North African campaign was followed by the invasions of Sicily and Italy, where the RAF Regiment continued to support air operations by defending RAF airfields against enemy ground and air attack, as well as by taking their place alongside Army units in the front line. RAF Regiment units were also engaged in operations against the Germans in the Balkans and in defeating the attempt to establish a communist regime in Greece. In the Far East the RAF Regiment enabled RAF aircraft to provide close support for the Army by operating from airstrips in the combat zone as the British steadily drove the Japanese out of Burma prior to the planned reoccupation of Malaya and Singapore. But the largest concentration of RAF Regiment forces was committed to North West Europe from D-Day onwards and played a major role in occupying and defending the airfields which the Second Tactical Air Force used as the Allied advance towards the German homeland brought the war in Europe to an end. Even at that late stage in the war the RAF Regiment played an important part in the home defence of the United Kingdom by deploying a large number of its anti-aircraft squadrons in the gun belt across southern England which, with fighter aircraft, countered the flying bomb assault which was intended to destroy London before Germany could be defeated.

At the end of the Second World War the RAF Regiment was little more than three years old but its achievements, in every part of the world in which the Royal Air Force operated against the enemy, had proved the essential contribution which its wings and squadrons made to the effectiveness of tactical air operations worldwide.

Its officers and airmen had learned their demanding trade quickly in the hard school of war, and the continuing existence of the RAF Regiment in the Royal Air Force's post-war order of battle is a tribute to the dedicated professionalism and courage of those who served in it from 1942 until the end of hostilities.

# PROLOGUE

"The only new thing in this world is the history you don't know"
Harry S Truman (1884-1972) President of the USA 1945-1952

On the morning of 8 November 1942 some of the troopships of
Convoy KM.1, loaded with the assault force for Operation *Torch* - the
Anglo-American invasion of French North Africa – hove to off the
beaches at Ain Taya, twenty miles east of the port of Algiers. It was a
cold, grey winter's morning and the ships rolled in the stiffening breeze
which was beginning to push the ocean swell into a foaming surf which
broke ominously on the deserted shoreline. Flight Lieutenants Searle
and Law, the respective commanders of Nos.4088 and 4089 Anti-
Aircraft Flights of the RAF Regiment, surveyed the scene with some
misgiving as their heavily-laden airmen clambered down the swaying
cargo nets into the landing craft which bumped and swayed alongside
the troopships. Their fears proved justified when the landing craft which
had put them ashore found the sea too rough to load their stores and
equipment for subsequent journeys from the ships to the beaches.

Stranded ashore, the troops watched with dismay as the convoy
weighed anchor and sailed for Algiers, leaving the officers and airmen of
the RAF Regiment to march to their objective – the airfield at Maison
Blanche, fifteen miles away. The following day, less than three months
after their formation in the Isle of Man and after more than a fortnight
at sea, they were reunited with their guns and vehicles on the crowded
and war-damaged docks at Algiers. Almost immediately 4088 Flight was
in action defending Maison Blanche against German air attacks while
4089 Flight was similarly occupied at Bone airfield. As the subsequent
Torch convoys reached Algeria in the following weeks, the RAF
Regiment front line in North Africa increased in strength to five field
squadrons and five AA flights, and by the time the campaign had moved
to Sicily and Italy in 1943 the RAF Regiment's order of battle in the
Central Mediterranean had risen to almost seven thousand men in
more than thirty field and LAA squadrons.

In Egypt, after the victory at El Alamein in October 1942, the 8th
Army and the Desert Air Force had begun their advance westwards
towards Tunis. The forward airfields used by wings and squadrons of
tactical aircraft were defended by the newly-raised AA flights of the
RAF Regiment which were in action against German aircraft until the
campaign ended in Tunis in May 1943. A rapid reorganization of the
eight thousand ground gunners already in the theatre and earmarked for
the RAF Regiment, enabled more formed combat units to be deployed

throughout the Middle East, as well as providing reinforcements for the Regiment forces in Sicily, Italy, the Balkans and Greece as the various campaigns in the Central Mediterranean developed.

In the Far East, where the Army and RAF had been thrown into disarray by the rapid Japanese advance through Malaya and into Burma in 1942, it took longer for the tide to turn and for RAF Regiment units to be formed from the four thousand ground gunners who were already in India. However, from 1943 onwards the Regiment's field and LAA squadrons were being deployed on forward airfields in Burma and by the time of the Japanese surrender over six thousand personnel in thirty Regiment squadrons were available to participate in the invasion of Malaya and Singapore prior to the recapture of Borneo, French Indo-China and the Dutch East Indies as part of the RAF's planned deployment to those areas.

In the United Kingdom 1942 was a hectic year for the RAF Regiment which was being organized, trained, equipped and deployed while at the same time preparing its operational units for reinforcement roles in the major theatres of war outside the UK and, indeed, in other operations wherever the Royal Air Force was engaged against the enemy. While over a hundred squadrons were assigned to home defence duties, some fifteen thousand men in another seventy-five squadrons were to be deployed in North-West Europe from D-Day until VE-Day, as part of the Second Tactical Air Force, where they made an essential contribution towards the tactical air operations which enabled the Allies to defeat the German forces in NW Europe.

For a force originally conceived as simply an airfield defence corps, the RAF Regiment expanded its capabilities into roles never envisaged by the Findlater Stewart Committee when it had considered the problems of airfield defence in 1941 and recommended the formation of the RAF Regiment. Nevertheless, despite such varied tasks as manning the guns on troop transports in convoys to airborne operations, coastal raiding as part of special forces, reconnaissance and operations alongside, and sometimes ahead of, the Army, the RAF Regiment always fulfilled its primary commitment to the RAF by defending air bases and forward installations against ground and air attack and by clearing and occupying forward airfields for RAF use as British forces advanced in every theatre of war from 1943 onwards.

This, then, is the story of a unique combat force and of the men who carried the RAF Regiment forward to play its part in the Second World War from 1942 until the post-war turmoil was thought to be at its end in 1946.

# CHAPTER ONE

# A TIME OF CHANGE

The War of 1914-1918 produced two significant advances in military technology: the combat aircraft and the armoured fighting vehicle. Neither had realized anything approaching their overwhelming influence on the battlefield by the time the war ended, but their appearance in the complex mechanism of warfare cast long shadows which were neither welcomed nor understood by many Service officers and politicians. Indeed, the Chief of the Imperial General Staff was quick to dismiss the newly-formed Royal Air Force as "coming from God knows where, dropping its bombs on God knows what, and going off God knows where". Those Army officers, such as Fuller and Hobart, who advocated the replacement of cavalry by armoured fighting vehicles were regarded as cranks by their professional colleagues and even the foremost military commentator of the day, Basil Liddell Hart, was ridiculed for his arguments for the "indirect approach" which advocated the use of armoured columns, supported by aircraft, to defeat an enemy army by striking at headquarters, communications and logistic support areas behind the conventional front line. But these theories fell on more fertile ground in the resurgent German General Staff where the *blitzkrieg* doctrine of fast-moving armoured columns combined with airborne operations and close air support was being developed and refined from Liddell Hart's pioneering ideas.

Just as Liddell Hart had analysed the future of war on land, another military mind had concentrated on establishing the principles of air power and the means of applying them in war. This was the Italian General Giulio Douhet, who published his treatise *The Command of the Air* in 1921, soon after the end of the First World War. In his remarkably perceptive study of the aims and methods of air warfare he revealed a principle of fundamental importance when he wrote "The surest and most effective way (of achieving air superiority) is to destroy the enemy air force at its bases" – a statement so obvious in itself that it escaped the attention of many of those in influential positions in the British political and military establishment. However, its significance did not escape the German High Command which was developing the strategy for a new form of warfare, based on modern technology which could effectively destroy any enemy unwise enough to believe that the next war would be won by using the methods which had prevailed in the previous one.

The Maginot Line came to be regarded as the modern answer to the debilitating siege warfare which had been the major feature of the Western Front from 1914 to 1918, and few of those who had experienced that conflict could visualize the developments in strategy and tactics which would make headquarters, airfields and supply depots in the rear areas much more vulnerable to the greater mobility and firepower of ground forces, and to a devastating level of attack from the air, than had been possible even in 1918. From the experience it had gained with the Royal Flying Corps, which was then a part of the Army, between 1914 and 1918 the War Office maintained the principle that, as war on land was the Army's responsibility, the Army should continue to provide and command the ground and anti-aircraft defences which the Royal Air Force required for the security of its airfields and installations. Despite the RAF's status as an independent Service, the Air Ministry was content to accept those assurances at their face value, without assessing the implications, in terms of limitations on its own freedom of action, on the conduct of air operations in a future conflict.

In the lean years after the First World War, when the Armed Forces were the poor relations in terms of government expenditure, there were few resources to spare either to develop new technology or to train for a major war. In those locust years both the Army and the RAF were committed to the policy of "imperial policing" in British colonial possessions, which usually took the form of aiding the civil power to restore law and order in urban areas of the Empire, or dealing with incursions and rebellions by lightly-armed tribesmen in the deserts of the Middle East and on the North-West Frontier of India. These activities placed minimal demands on the development of weapons and tactics for a major war and it was hardly surprising that, despite a frantic rearmament programme from 1936 to the outbreak of war in 1939, the British armed forces lagged far behind their enemies in terms of the organization, tactical doctrine, training, weapons and equipment essential for fighting a global war against major European and Asian powers.

In the inter-war years the British Army had struggled to come to terms with the implications of mobility and the employment of armoured fighting vehicles, but it was hampered by a lack of political and strategic direction as well as by inadequate resources. As far as the RAF was concerned, it was required to spread its limited capabilities between defending the United Kingdom against air attack, supporting the operations of the Army and the Royal Navy and in developing an offensive bomber force. In meeting this multiplicity of tasks, the Air Force had been assured that, by operating its aircraft from bases within the Army's area of responsibility, its airfields would be secure from enemy interference. What neither Service had taken into account was whether the Army would be able to fulfil such a complex and demanding commitment to the Royal Air Force in the yet unrevealed scenario of modern war.

However, as the prospect of another conflict with Germany became more likely, the more thoughtful members of the Air Staff began to appreciate the dangers inherent in relying on another Service, which had different roles and priorities, for the defence of its own airfields and vital installations. Initially, the threat was seen simply as one of low-level air attack by enemy aircraft which had evaded the RAF's defensive fighter screen and no serious thought was given to the possibility of direct attack on airfields by ground or airborne forces.

To cater for defence against low level air attack, for which neither funding nor new weapons had been provided, searches in the RAF's supply depots revealed that a number of surplus, First World War vintage, aircraft machine guns still remained in store. These were adapted for use in the defence of airfields and a number of airmen in the trade of Aircrafthand General Duties (ACH/GD) were given cursory training in the handling of these weapons against low-flying aircraft. It was a half-hearted attempt to make bricks without straw and, when put to the test in France and Norway in 1940, it failed miserably. The RAF's improvised airfield defence measures were swept aside as its forward airfields were strafed by the Luftwaffe and outflanked or overrun by the panzers of the Wehrmacht as the Germans swept through France, the Low Countries and parts of Scandinavia. Despite the gallantry of RAF aircrews, the battle for air superiority was lost as airfields in the forward areas were abandoned and aircraft in the rear areas were destroyed on the ground by a German tactical air force engaged in proving the validity of Douhet's analysis of the fundamentals of air warfare.

The Luftwaffe was essentially an integrated air arm, with its own infantry, airborne and air defence artillery units, which had little difficulty in achieving air superiority in the early stages of the war by the simple expedient of neutralizing the enemy's air bases while its own airfields were well protected against attack by its own infantry and anti-aircraft units. However, after winning the Battles of Poland, France and Norway by such tactics, the Germans failed to win the Battle of Britain, largely because the English Channel protected the British airfields from ground attack while the elementary radar system on the south and east coasts of England gave adequate warning time for British fighter aircraft to be airborne from their lightly-defended airfields before the waves of attacking aircraft crossed the English Channel. Elsewhere in the United Kingdom, where radar warning and airfield defences were more limited or even non-existent, German air attacks in broad daylight achieved far greater success. RAF airfields, without adequate defences, were attacked with impunity from Wick and Lossiemouth in Scotland through Driffield, Leeming and Dishforth in the North of England to Castle Bromwich and Kirton-in-Lindsey in the Midlands and Kidlington, Mildenhall and Honington in the south and east.

It was at this point that it became all too clear that the RAF's ability to fight – and win – the air war would depend on the protection provided for its bases against hostile action by enemy ground and air forces. Inevitably, the threat of an imminent invasion after Dunkirk in 1940 caused the Army to give priority to the land battle over the defence of RAF airfields and it became increasingly obvious to the Air Staff that, under the pressures of war, the interests and capabilities of the two Services were diverging to such an extent that the RAF would have to rely on its own resources to ensure that its installations would survive attack and retain the capability for its aircraft to operate effectively against the enemy.

In July 1940, even before the evacuation of British forces from the European mainland was complete, the Air Ministry formed the RAF's Directorate of Ground Defence to co-ordinate the ground and anti-aircraft defence of airfields and installations with the Army's Inspectorate of Aerodrome Defence. In August 1940, realizing the extent and urgency of the problem, Air Chief Marshal Sir Frederick Bowhill advocated the formation of a ground defence corps, modelled on the Royal Marines, within the RAF and this proposal was strongly supported by the Deputy Chief of Air Staff, Air Marshal Sir Sholto Douglas. There was inevitable opposition to this within the War Office, as well as in some parts of the Royal Air Force, and the pessimistic estimates of the additional manpower which this would require – up to 100,000 men – doomed the project at a time when all three Services were competing for the limited resources of manpower and material which were then available in the UK.

The compromise solution was to continue the patchwork division of responsibility between the Army and the Air Force for the ground and air defence of RAF airfields and installations in the United Kingdom by a mixed force of 17,000 soldiers and 25,000 airmen. The RAF element of this force consisted of NCOs and aircraftmen (remustered in the new trade of Ground Gunner from mid-1940 onwards), officered by the Defence specialization of the Administrative & Special Duties branch. However, although the deployment of the RAF component of this mixed force remained relatively stable, the Army inevitably altered the number, type and strength of its assigned units to meet the recurring changes in the deployment of its anti-invasion forces. This made the planning and direction of airfield defences difficult, if not impossible, particularly as the War Office always insisted that local Army commanders retained the right to redeploy their units elsewhere, without notice, whenever the overall military situation required it and regardless of the level of ground and air threats to the maintenance of aircraft operations. The result was that RAF commanders had to accept that their airfields would be left without the protection of Army units whenever the Army required reinforcements for the land battle, regardless of the threat to airfields and the maintenance of air operations.

Although station defence measures were still at an early stage of development, there were a series of successful anti-aircraft engagements during attacks on RAF airfields in England from July 1940 to the formation of the RAF Regiment in early 1942. During the Battle of Britain, for instance, at RAF Detling Corporal Bruce Jackman continued firing his twin Lewis guns at attacking aircraft until his gun position was demolished by a bomb and he was severely wounded. At RAF Biggin Hill Sergeant Robert Cunningham dismounted a machine gun from an armoured car and engaged three enemy aircraft which were bombing the airfield. At RAF Kenley Corporal John Miller of the Scots Guards shot down a German aircraft with his Lewis gun, while AC2 David Roberts destroyed another enemy aircraft by using the RAF's newest anti-aircraft weapon for the first time. This was the parachute-and-cable system in which a line of twenty-five rockets was fired in the path of attacking aircraft. The rockets soared to a height of 500 feet, each trailing a steel cable attached to a parachute and the spectacular display of smoke and flames heartened the British defenders on the ground as much as it dismayed the German aircrew as two of the three attacking Dornier 17 bombers were brought down. All three RAF airmen, and the Scots Guards NCO, were awarded Military Medals for their actions. Other awards to RAF Ground Gunners in this period included two George Medals, two more Military Medals, five British Empire Medals for gallantry, seven mentions in dispatches and a King's Commendation for Brave Conduct.

As training, equipment and organization of airfield defence improved throughout 1941, the Ground Gunner anti-aircraft flights achieved steadily increasing success against those enemy aircraft which attacked

RAF airfields and installations at low level. What was universally recognized, however, was that a better and more effective anti-aircraft weapon than the .303″ machine gun was needed to improve the kill rate – and the deterrent effect – of airfield defences.

Although the effectiveness of anti-aircraft defences on RAF airfields in the UK declined as the emphasis of German strategy changed from daylight raids at low level to high-altitude night bombing attacks, the unabated success of enemy action against RAF airfields in the Middle East revealed the many weaknesses in the policy of dividing the responsibility for airfield defence between two Services with different priorities. The last straw, as far as the War Cabinet was concerned, was the unsuccessful British campaign in Greece in 1941, culminating in the fall of Crete and the loss of most of the British, New Zealand and Greek troops who had been evacuated there from Greece, together with their weapons and equipment. There were three airfields on the northern coast of Crete, at Maleme, near Canae on the west, at Retimo in the centre and at Heraklion in the east, as well as a flying boat base at Suda Bay. Maleme was the closest to the German bases in Greece and had the added advantage of being adjacent to a large town and the port at Suda Bay; it was therefore the enemy's primary objective. The initial assault by glider-borne and parachute troops was disastrously expensive for the Germans but by concentrating their resources on the single objective of Maleme they were able to capture the airfield within 48 hours. From then onwards a stream of transport aircraft, each carrying forty fully-armed men or an equivalent load of supplies, was landing at the rate of up to twenty an hour and the British garrison, without air support or reinforcement, was overwhelmed.

In the United Kingdom the much greater awareness of the importance of air power directed attention to the security of airfields in concert with the introduction of new aircraft. In Parliament pressure for a speedy resolution of the problem of airfield defence became overwhelming and the government was forced to appoint a distinguished civil servant, Sir Findlater Stewart, to head a committee tasked to examine ways of improving airfield defence and to submit its report to the Chiefs of Staff within the shortest possible time. The committee's recommendation that the RAF should form its own airfield defence corps of 79,000 officers and airmen, which would release 93,000 soldiers from airfield defence tasks, was accepted by the War Office and the Air Ministry, and approved by the War Cabinet in December 1941. As a result, the War Office agreed to give full support to the new organization by providing instructors, weapons and equipment as well as by seconding officers and NCOs to serve with the RAF Regiment.

HM King George VI gave his formal assent to the formation of this Corps, as an integral part of the Royal Air Force, by a Royal Warrant signed on 6 January 1942 and the Royal Air Force Regiment duly came into existence on 1 February 1942.

By building on the structure of the officers in the defence specialization of the Administrative & Special Duties branch and the NCOs and aircraftmen of the Ground Gunner trade, the new Regiment reached a strength of 50,000 officers and airmen in 240 combatant squadrons, which were deployed alongside the RAF in every theatre of war, within 18 months of its formation.

# CHAPTER TWO

# THE FORMATION OF THE RAF
# REGIMENT

In January 1942 there were 150 RAF ground defence squadrons and
335 RAF independent anti-aircraft flights deployed on RAF stations in
the British Isles. They had been formed during 1941 in response to the
enemy threat to RAF airfields and were officered by those members of
the Administrative & Special Duties branch of the RAF who had been
trained as Defence Officers, and manned by NCOs and aircraftmen
mustered as Ground Gunners, most of whom were drawn from the
trade of Aircrafthand General Duties.

Although the ground defence squadrons were based on the model
of an Army infantry company, they had only personal weapons and
lacked the heavier support weapons with which the infantry units
were equipped. The anti-aircraft flights were scaled for between
twelve and twenty-four .303″ machine guns of various types on a
variety of mountings, but these did not present a real deterrent, let
alone a serious threat, to enemy aircraft attacking at anything other
than very low level within a few hundred yards of a static anti-aircraft
machine-gun position.

With the formation of the RAF Regiment on 1 February 1942 the
Army fulfilled its commitment to provide a cadre of officer and NCO
instructors at the newly formed training schools, as well as providing
senior officers to fill staff posts in the Air Ministry and at RAF
Command and Group headquarters. Although the Vice-Chief of Air
Staff had asked for a lieutenant-general to head the new Regiment, the
War Office considered that to be an over-ambitious rank for the
appointment and seconded Major-General Claude Liardet, who was
already the Army's Inspector of Aerodrome Defence, to take the post
of Commandant of the RAF Regiment. A Territorial, not a Regular,
Army officer, Liardet had a distinguished record in the 1914-18 war
and had been the General Officer Commanding the London TA
Division in 1939.

In March 1942 the RAF Regiment Depot was established at Lord
Brownlow's country seat, Belton Park, near Grantham, and a separate
RAF Regiment officer cadet training unit was formed there to produce
officers with the necessary professional skills. Numerous instructional

*RAF Regiment OCTU, RAF Regiment Depot Belton Park, September 1944. The Commandant of the Depot, Air Commodore Higgins CB CMG, and the reviewing Air Marshal are looking closely at Officer Cadet Roland George (on the extreme right of the picture).* (R George)

schools were established to carry out basic and advanced training and several live firing ranges were designated for ground and anti-aircraft weapons. The training task was immense: for a start all the officers and airmen in the existing squadrons and flights had to be retrained as individuals to higher military standards appropriate to their roles and ranks before they could be trained collectively in flights and squadrons for combat tasks.

The overloaded training machine received welcome assistance from the Royal Marines, who undertook much of the task of training the Regiment's own NCO instructors, while a number of officer and NCO instructors provided by the Brigade of Guards ensured that the initial training of airmen reached a sufficiently high standard. The contribution which instructors from these two elite formations made to the foundation of the RAF Regiment was immense and to this day the RAF Regiment maintains its links with the training establishments of both the Guards Division and the Corps of Royal Marines.

Inevitably, a significant number of officers and airmen were found to be medically unfit or below the standards required for the new Regiment during this phase and had to be replaced by transfers from other RAF trades and by intakes of new recruits. As unit weapons, including anti-tank artillery, mortars and 20mm anti-aircraft guns, and unit equipment such as MT vehicles and armoured cars, were in short supply, improvisation was the order of the day. Nevertheless, by June 1942 there were 148 fully-trained and operational field squadrons available and by June 1943 the formation of new field squadrons and the reorganization of the former AA flights into LAA squadrons had increased the Regiment's order of battle to some 40,000 officers and airmen in 240 squadrons in the United Kingdom, the Mediterranean, Middle East and Far East. With the addition of staff appointments, instructors and personnel under training, the RAF Regiment reached its wartime peak of 50,000 officers and men in July 1943.

As the operational squadrons were deployed in their war roles at home and overseas, the need for more effective armament became even more pressing. The standard British small arms, the No.4 rifle and the Bren light machine gun, were made available in sufficient quantities to equip personnel in the field squadrons but there was a grave shortage of support weapons. The first of these to be issued to field squadrons in the United Kingdom, the Smith gun, was an improvised smooth-bore weapon which fired modified 3″ mortar bombs and was reputed to be more dangerous to its users than to the enemy. Because of that, replacements for it were gratefully received, whatever they were and whenever they became available. These included 75mm howitzers left over from the 1914-18 war, obsolescent 2 pounder anti-tank guns and, for a short while in North Africa, surplus 25 pounder field guns loaned by the Army, which were later replaced by 6 pounder anti-tank guns. Eventually, this motley range of support weapons was superseded solely by the 3″ medium mortar which became the standard weapon in the support flights of the field squadrons.

The independent AA flights were established for twin Browning machine guns on anti-aircraft mountings, but these were often replaced or augmented by obsolescent Lewis or Vickers guns, sometimes in quadruple mountings, in an effort to boost the firepower of the anti-aircraft defences. However, from 1943 onwards 20mm Hispano cannons, on anti-aircraft mountings, began to replace the

.303″ machine guns and gave the LAA units the greater capability which they badly needed.

The first attempts at structuring the establishments of the Regiment's combat units were obscured by the imagined need to match unit capabilities to a variety of roles and the results seemed to bear out the old adage that a camel is a horse which has been designed by a committee. There were to be no less than three types of field squadron: the 'standard' field squadron had an anti-aircraft flight, two rifle flights – only one of which was 'mobile' – a support flight and an armoured car flight; the 'higher' field squadron had a third rifle flight added, while the 'lower' field squadron had only the anti-aircraft flight and two rifle flights. There were also two other versions of the so-called 'independent' anti-aircraft flight: the 'special' flight consisted of half a rifle flight and two anti-aircraft half-flights, whereas the 'composite' flight was composed of three half-flights, each of riflemen, anti-aircraft guns and armoured cars.

Fortunately, this confusing pattern was swept away by common sense in October 1942, after which only two basic types of unit remained in being: the field squadron of seven officers and 178 airmen grouped in three rifle flights, a support weapons flight and an armoured car flight, and the independent anti-aircraft flight of two officers and fifty-eight airmen manning anti-aircraft machine guns, which were later replaced by 20mm Hispano cannons. The independent AA flights in the UK, the Middle East and the Mediterranean were formed into LAA squadrons of eight officers and 162 airmen from May 1943 onwards, and were progressively re-equipped with Bofors 40mm guns to replace the 20mm Hispanos. In the Far East, however, the shortage of Bofors 40mm guns resulted in the retention of the 20mm Hispano gun as the standard weapon of the LAA squadrons in that theatre until the end of the war.

In 1944 an appraisal of the role of the Regiment in the forthcoming invasion of North-West Europe was made following the experience gained in the campaigns in the Middle East. This led to a further reorganization of the field squadrons assigned to the Second Tactical Air Force which involved removing their armoured car flights and concentrating the flights in separate armoured car squadrons, leaving the truncated field squadrons to be designated as rifle squadrons, each with three rifle flights and a support weapons flight of 3″ mortars. The Mediterranean campaign had proved that command and control of two or more squadrons operating together in the field required a wing headquarters to control them operationally, and a number of such headquarters were established in the United Kingdom on the lines of those which were already in being in overseas theatres.

Although the structure of the RAF Regiment was subject to constant change in its early days, it soon evolved into the effective fighting force which was required to fulfil the RAF's requirements for the ground and low-level air defence of its airfields and vital installations such as radar units. However, a series of problems arose in integrating such an organization into the RAF's command and staff structure, which had, of course, developed to deal with the conduct of air warfare in isolation from ground and low level air defence, and few RAF officers had sufficient understanding of the value of the new RAF Regiment in its important role of supporting tactical air operations.

Apart from the fact that many Air Force commanders had little training or experience in the conduct of war on land, most of the RAF officers, who, for the first time, had control of their own ground defence forces, lacked the motivation or imagination to employ them effectively. This was not helped by the original decision to categorize the Regiment in an administrative role, as providing a service to the operational branch and thus reducing its effectiveness in formulating the development of operational policy. Although this unsatisfactory situation was later rectified by placing the Regiment's responsibilities within the Air Staff division, the most senior Regiment officers who could exercise operational control on the ground were the squadron leaders who commanded Regiment squadrons until, later in the war, Regiment wing headquarters were established to exercise control of between two and five squadrons, depending on the operational situation at the time. More senior Regiment officers were restricted to the staffs of group or command headquarters, where they had only an advisory role, and although as staff officers within the Air Staff they had greater access to operational planning, they still had no direct control over RAF Regiment units, which remained under the immediate command of station commanders, normally of the General Duties branch, who were primarily concerned with aircraft operations.

Not surprisingly, this system often resulted in the misuse or misemployment of the necessarily limited Regiment resources in the Air Force. At best, it led to Regiment personnel being employed on a variety of mundane tasks quite unrelated to their training and experience; at worst, there were to be instances when under-strength Regiment units were committed piecemeal, or in small numbers, to operations in which they were inevitably outnumbered by superior enemy forces, of whose capabilities the RAF commanders, or their staff officers, were all too often unaware. Of course there were exceptions to this, particularly as the war progressed and when hard lessons had been learned from experience. In contrast, senior Army commanders were never backward in asking the RAF for Regiment squadrons to support Army units in operations against enemy ground forces in NW Europe, the Middle East and the Far East. When deployed under command of the Army in these theatres, the Regiment squadrons invariably received high praise for their professional skills in action from the senior officers of the battalions, brigades and divisions under whose command they were placed.

Inevitably, the results of this amorphous organization were directly related to the leadership, training and combat skills of the officers, non-commissioned officers and airmen of the RAF Regiment, particularly when they were in key positions at critical places and at critical times. With less than four years of war in which to develop from its formation, there was not much opportunity for those officers with purely RAF Regiment backgrounds to make a significant impact on events, even though many of them displayed above-average professional ability in staff and unit appointments up to the rank of wing commander, as the majority of the more senior posts were inevitably held by officers seconded from the Army. Furthermore, as senior staff officers at the major RAF headquarters, many competent Army officers shaped the operational successes of the RAF Regiment by their involvement in planning and directing the employment of wings and squadrons during the war.

In the Air Ministry Major-General Claude Liardet, who became the RAF's Director-General of Ground Defence and Commandant of the RAF Regiment in February 1942, ensured a smooth interface between the Army and the Air Force wherever their ground and low-level air defence tasks overlapped. He and his staff officers were equally concerned with the organization, training, equipment and deployment of the RAF Regiment as a whole and his achievements were recognized by the award of a knighthood before the war ended.

Colonel Morrey Salmon was selected to be the senior RAF Regiment officer in the force which was assembled for Operation *Torch*, the invasion of North Africa in November 1942. He broke new ground by refusing to remain simply a staff officer in the North African Air Force Headquarters and appointed himself "Commander RAF Regiment" and as such had a decisive effect on the peformance of the wings and squadrons of the RAF Regiment which served in the ensuing campaigns in Sicily, Italy, the Balkans and Greece between 1943 and 1945.

Colonel J. B. Rosher displayed his keen legal mind as head of the RAF Regiment staff in the Middle East, where he was responsible for large-scale reorganization and retraining followed by the deployment of operational units to the airfields of the Desert Air Force. Once the battle moved to Sicily and then Italy, he ensured the steady flow of reinforcing units to the Central Mediterranean.

In the Far East Group Captain Jack Harris became the Command Defence Officer at Air Headquarters India in late 1942 with the remit to reorganize the fragmented RAF Regiment resources into formed units and establish a coherent airfield defence structure in the theatre. A former pilot and infantry officer, the combination of his military experience and a natural aptitude for staff work ensured that, within the shortest possible period of time, RAF Regiment units were trained, equipped and deployed on forward airfields in Assam and Burma. Integrated into 221 and 224 Groups of the 3rd Tactical Air Force, they made an invaluable contribution to the success of air operations against the Japanese army and its air arm.

The main theatre of operations was, however, North-West Europe, where the majority of the Regiment's wings and squadrons were deployed within the Second Tactical Air Force in which an experienced infantry officer, Brigadier M. A. Green, was the head of the RAF Regiment staff. Each of the four groups within 2TAF had its own RAF Regiment staff officers as well, at either colonel or lieutenant-colonel level, and this ensured that policy and operations were integrated and effective throughout the campaign in Europe. In 2TAF at least, the importance of the RAF Regiment's contribution was clearly appreciated by RAF commanders and the Regiment's wings and squadrons were effectively employed in a variety of essential operational tasks in support of air operations throughout the campaign, culminating in the occupation of the whole of Schleswig-Holstein for HQ 2TAF before the war ended.

CHAPTER THREE

# EVENTS IN THE UNITED KINGDOM

With the formation of the RAF Regiment in February 1942 the Army's post of Inspector of Aerodrome Defence at the War Office became redundant and Major-General Liardet moved to the Air Ministry to take up the twin posts of Director-General of Ground Defence (RAF) and Commandant of the RAF Regiment. The Directorate of Ground Defence, which had existed in the Air Ministry since 1940, was expanded to include staff officers from both the Army and the RAF: Air Commodore A. P. Ledger succeeded Air Commodore A. P. M. Sanders as the Director of Ground Defence and Major-General Liardet's deputy, while the post of Deputy Director of Ground Defence was filled by an experienced soldier, Colonel the Lord Bingham, late of the Grenadier Guards.

The task of creating a new operational structure in the midst of a war in which practically every resource was in short supply was a formidable one, but it was tackled with diligence and energy under the new management. The existing 150 ground defence squadrons and the 335 AA flights were renumbered as RAF Regiment units and reorganized and trained for their new combatant roles. Unit establishments were revised and equipment and weaponry updated wherever possible in order to meet the requirement to deploy field squadrons at 147 RAF stations and anti-aircraft flights at 329 airfields. The first RAF Regiment wing commanders on operational units were authorized as early as March 1942 when these posts were established on stations where two or more Regiment squadrons were deployed. Functional wing headquarters had not been envisaged at this time and these wing commanders had to operate without supporting staff in co-ordinating the activities of their squadrons, many of which still lacked uniformity in manning or equipment. As an example, 2703 Field Squadron at RAF Merston had an interesting scale of unit weapons at this time: six Beaverette armoured cars, four Smith guns, two 75mm field guns and three light tanks, which had been acquired from the Royal Tank Regiment. Fortunately, most of the Canadian .300″ Ross rifles which had been issued as a stopgap, had been replaced by the British .303″ Enfield rifle as the standard personal weapon, which was helpful, as the British and Canadian ammunition was not interchangeable.

It was decided that the RAF Regiment, as an integral part of the Royal Air Force, would follow RAF precedent as far as possible; the only immediate concession was that for practical reasons khaki, and not air force blue, uniforms would be worn by those serving in operational units. Similarly, the traditional RAF forage cap, as worn by officers and airmen of other branches and trades, was unsuitable for field operations and was progressively replaced by the issue of a new air force blue beret for all ranks of the Regiment.

The recommendations of the Findlater Stewart Committee, which led to the formation of the Regiment, included the establishment of 79,000 officers and airmen in the United Kingdom; when the requirements of the RAF in overseas theatres were taken into account, a further 14,000 men were added, a total force level of 93,000 all ranks for the RAF Regiment. Given the overriding demand for manpower in all three Services, this was clearly an unattainable figure and it was very soon amended to a total of 85,000 – 75,000 in the UK and 10,000 overseas. By December 1942 the establishment had been further reduced to a total of 47,000 at home and 10,000 overseas and in July 1943 the size of the Regiment was fixed at 50,000 all ranks – 39,000 in the UK and 11,000 overseas. This was, in fact, a sensible figure in terms of the RAF's requirement and the availability of recruits, but it was to be eroded later by the Army's insistence on obtaining airmen from the Air Force to fill shortfalls in its own units. The paper strength of the Regiment had actually peaked at 53,000 in late 1942, but several thousand of these were non-effectives, inherited from the original defence squadrons, who had been assessed as either medically unfit or unsuitable for retraining, and were awaiting remustering to other less active RAF trades. However, by July 1943 240 field and LAA squadrons were operational in the United Kingdom, the Mediterranean and the Far East.

Despite the shortage of experienced officers and senior NCOs, the training and reorganization of squadrons and flights proceeded rapidly. 148 field squadrons and 290 anti-aircraft flights reached operational status by the end of 1942, although there were shortages of weapons and equipment which made it difficult, if not impossible, for all units to be equipped to the standard scales.

The danger of the lack of adequate supervision based on military experience in an environment in which realistic training was carried out with enthusiasm was illustrated by an incident involving 2716 Squadron during a station defence exercise at RAF Skitten in April 1942. A platoon of 9th Seaforth Highlanders was acting as enemy when one of the squadron airmen challenged an intruder who was in civilian clothes. The intruder's response was to draw a pistol and order his challenger to surrender – unfortunately, the defender, who for some unexplained reason had live ammunition in his rifle, promptly shot and wounded the intruder, who turned out to be Lieutenant McKenzie of the Seaforths. His platoon subsequently ambushed the 2716 Squadron airman who had fired the shot and beat him up so severely that he was hospitalized for several weeks.

In 1941 the Air Ministry had ordered 2,000 Smith guns, instead of the 40mm Bofors guns which, although the preferred choice, were unavailable at that time, even though field trials indicated that light machine guns and .50″ anti-tank rifles were more effective than an untried and improvised weapon. The Smith gun was the invention of Major W. H. Smith, the managing director of Trianco Toys, and was intended as a smooth-bore substitute for an artillery piece. It fired a modified 3″ mortar bomb against ground targets at ranges of up to 1,600 yards, but subsequent attempts to increase this to 3,000 yards had to be abandoned due to the excessive recoil and instability which this generated. Production problems with fuzes delayed the introduction of the weapons until 1942, but it was not long before the first fatal accident occurred. During a live firing practice in that year a malfunction caused an explosion which killed Corporal Maynard of 2819 Squadron. Other such incidents soon followed and after a very unsatisfactory operational performance, and a worse safety record, in squadron service, all Smith guns were withdrawn from Regiment units in 1943.

There were a number of different marks of Beaverette armoured cars within the RAF but these were not ideal for the field squadrons' roles, even after the Mk IIIs were rearmed with twin Vickers machine guns in June 1942. The situation improved as the Beaverettes were replaced with Morris and Humber 4x4 armoured cars as these became available. Once the latter types were in squadron service it became clear that they had the potential to contribute far more to the Regiment's operational effectiveness if they were grouped into independent armoured car squadrons instead of being distributed in small numbers throughout the field squadron establishment. This was to lead to a further unit reorganization shortly before D-Day.

The RAF Regiment Depot and RAF Regiment OCTU were co-located at Belton Park and training schools for NCOs and airmen were established at Filey, Whitley Bay, Ronaldsway, Locking and Hednesford. Regional ground defence training centres were also opened at Arbroath, Skegness and Hereford. The artillery school for field, anti-tank and anti-aircraft gunnery was at Eastchurch and no fewer than seventeen anti-aircraft ranges throughout the United Kingdom were utilized for training courses and by anti-aircraft flights. The school instructors were initially provided by the Army and the Royal Marines but the aim was to select and train RAF Regiment personnel to replace them at the various training schools without undue delay, as well as to turn out personnel of all ranks who were qualified to take their places in operational units.

While the Directorate of Ground Defence in the Air Ministry was almost fully occupied in 1942 with planning the details of Regiment organization, equipment, training and operational deployment within the United Kingdom, the concurrent development of Operation *Torch*, the Allied invasion of French North Africa, scheduled for November 1942, added another dimension to the tasking of RAF Regiment units. The requirement was for five field squadrons and five independent anti-aircraft flights to be prepared for embarkation with the invasion fleet in October 1942, only eight months after the Regiment had come into existence. In addition, another 1,600 Regiment officers and men were added to the RAF contingent and distributed among the six wings of aircraft which were to operate from captured French airfields in Algeria. The senior Regiment officer appointed to this force of some 2,800 Regiment officers and airmen was a seconded Army lieutenant-colonel, equivalent in rank to a wing commander. The Regiment element of the Torch invasion force was not only trained and equipped within the required timescale but also distinguished itself in the North African campaign which began in Algiers in November 1942 and ended in victory in Tunis in May 1943.

The output of the various RAF Regiment training establishments

*RAF Regiment NCO instructors at the RAF Initial Training School, Heaton Park: Corporals Sayle, Hawkes, Rollitt and Grice in 1944.* (R Rollitt)

*Smith Gun training in the United Kingdom.* (Crown Copyright/MOD)

was not limited to filling the ranks of the Regiment's operational squadrons and flights. At Whitley Bay some of the new NCOs were retained as instructors and in October 1942 the newly-promoted Corporal Rollitt became an instructor in the aircrew escape and evasion wing. The training areas in Northumberland were bleak at the best of times and Australian aircrew who found themselves there in the winter months were even more disillusioned with the English weather than their British counterparts. Corporal Rollitt carried this work on at the RAF's aircrew initial training school at Heaton Park, near Manchester, and later at the training schools at Bridgnorth and Stormy Down. His particular Regiment instructional team finished its wartime service with a flourish by training the Flying Training Command contingent for the Victory Parade in London in 1945.

In February 1942 AC2 Scott of 2793 Squadron became the first of a series of Regiment personnel who displayed gallantry in connection with rescues from crashed aircraft. He was mentioned in despatches for his action in rescuing the pilot of a burning aircraft which crashed near Grantham.

By the beginning of 1943 airmen manning in the Regiment had improved but there was still a serious shortage of officers and the gap was filled by inviting experienced Army officers to apply for secondment or transfer to the Regiment. Almost 500 captains and majors, who were mostly overage for combatant service in the Army, were selected from a large number of candidates and most were employed in squadrons or as

*RAF Regiment officers on 166 OCTU course, RAF Jurby, 1942.* (R Cox)

advisers on RAF stations. A number of lieutenant-colonels and colonels had already been provided by the Army to act as senior defence advisers at RAF command and group headquarters and, as the Regiment component of 2TAF began to take shape, some of these officers were used to fill vacancies for commanders of operational wings and as staff officers in the four groups which made up 2TAF.

In March 1943 the independent AA flights, by then largely equipped with 20mm Hispano cannons, were reorganized into LAA squadrons which were intended to be re-equipped with the much more effective Bofors 40mm guns as they became available when personnel of the LAA regiments of the Royal Artillery were transferred from Anti-Aircraft Command to the infantry role in the field army. Unfortunately, the expected number of Bofors guns did not materialize and many of the newly-formed LAA squadrons had to make do with a less effective mixture of two flights of eight 20mm Hispanos and one flight of six 40mm Bofors. But the squadrons earmarked for 2TAF, and the forthcoming campaign in Europe, were issued with a full complement of twelve Bofors guns each.

As the weather improved in the spring of 1943 the Luftwaffe began a series of low-level 'tip-and-run' attacks on towns along the south coast of England. A number of LAA squadrons were deployed along the coast from Folkestone to Torquay (one with a detachment in the Scilly Isles) to engage attacking aircraft. These defences were, inevitably, thinly spread and the gun detachments were without mutual support so that attacking aircraft could only be engaged by a single anti-aircraft gun. Ronald Gullen Beales recalls that when his squadron was redeployed from Scampton to the Dymchurch/Hythe area in April 1943 his flight of 20mm Hispano guns was scattered along the coastline, out of sight, and out of range, of each other. To enable rapid reinforcement of likely lines of approach by enemy aircraft to possible targets, a further four anti-aircraft squadrons (2871 to 2874) were formed at the Regiment Depot and equipped with vehicle-mounted Browning machine guns before being deployed to the south coast. 2737 Squadron at Eastbourne and 2814 Squadron at Torquay were among others which shot down enemy aircraft and the robust defensive measures provided by the Regiment squadrons acted as a deterrent to more Luftwaffe raids on coastal towns.

The LAA squadrons were active in other areas: in July 1943 2731 Squadron destroyed a Dornier 217 bomber which attacked RAF Catfoss, while at large fighter airfields the Regiment squadrons combined LAA defence with rearming and refuelling Spitfires between sorties. At Martlesham Heath 2735 Squadron were involved in refuelling and rearming aircraft, while at Bradwell Bay in November 1943 the airmen of 2739 Squadron turned 132 Spitfires around in one day and on another day they refuelled and rearmed four complete Spitfire squadrons. At the same airfield, from July 1943 onwards, 2840 Squadron turned round a total of 3,572 Spitfire aircraft over a period of six months. At Merston in August 1943 2765 Squadron were occupied in refuelling and rearming three Spitfire squadrons while at Swanton Morley 2836 Squadron demonstrated its flexibility by bombing-up 226 (Bomber) Squadron's aircraft before they took off to attack targets in Europe.

At West Malling in April 1943 a Beaverette Mk III armoured car of 2769 Field Squadron was carrying out routine patrolling of the airfield at night when a German FW190 landed without warning on the main runway. The driver of the Beaverette, AC Wilding, immediately swung his vehicle in front of the aircraft to prevent it taking off and the two-man crew took the crestfallen NCO pilot prisoner. Driving back to the airfield from the guardroom, they saw a second FW190 land but, before the armoured car could reach it, the pilot realized his mistake and turned his aircraft round to begin his take-off run. The car commander, LAC Sharback, at once opened fire with his twin Vickers machine guns and the German aircraft slewed off the runway and caught fire. The pilot, wounded in the leg and shoulder and with his flying suit in flames, was thrown clear of the aircraft as it overturned. The two Regiment airmen ran to the German officer's rescue, extinguished his burning clothing and dragged him clear of the aircraft. Unfortunately, when one of the station's fire trucks was attempting to quench the flames the aircraft exploded in a ball of fire, scattering debris over a radius of three hundred yards and seriously injuring several of the RAF firemen. Within a few minutes another FW190 crashed on the approach to the runway while attempting to land and a fourth ploughed into a nearby orchard and burst into flames. These aircraft were part of an intruder force tasked to attack bombers returning from Germany as they landed at their home airfields, but many of the German single-seat fighters encountered navigational problems over the UK at night, ran short of fuel and attempted to land wherever they could.

Later that year an RAF aircraft crashed on the airfield at Hurn and caught fire. LAC Giles and AC Waites of 2796 Squadron were the first on the scene and were instrumental in rescuing members of the aircrew. For their actions the two Regiment airmen were each awarded the British Empire Medal.

The LAA squadrons defending radar stations on the Channel coast were able to contribute, albeit indirectly, to operations against the enemy as the radar stations at Swingate and Hawkshill Down were operating the Oboe system which enabled RAF and USAAF bombers to deliver precision bombing attacks on targets in NW Europe and Germany. When German attempts to jam the British radars failed, and low-level air attacks were foiled by 2725, 2728 and 2948 LAA Squadrons at Swingate and 2752 LAA Squadron at Hawkshill Down, the German long-range guns on the French coast attempted to neutralize the sites by periodic shelling, which sometimes lasted for up to twelve hours at a time. Although the heavily protected sites were not seriously damaged by the German shells, the blast from the explosions, and the shock waves from the British heavy coastal guns near Dover which retaliated, were uncomfortable for the radar operators and the Regiment gunners alike.

By this time it had become accepted policy to include Regiment units wherever aircraft were deployed to airfields which could be threatened by enemy ground or air attack. In 1943 agreement was reached with the Portuguese government for the stationing of Coastal Command aircraft in the Azores in order to close the mid-Atlantic gap where German U-boats were operating against Allied shipping, beyond the range of maritime patrol aircraft based in Britain or Canada. RAF Force 131, under the command of AVM Bromet, included 2710 Field Squadron when it sailed for the Azores in the converted liner Franconia from Liverpool in October 1943. Reaching the island of Terceira, the airfield

*2710 Field Squadron formed up at Lagens airfield, on the island of Terceira, in the Azores in 1944.* (PRO)

at Lagens, in the north-eastern corner of the island, was secured by the squadron and the components of a major operational airfield were assembled to provide surveillance over vast areas of the North Atlantic which had hitherto been inaccessible to the RAF.

The role of 2710 Squadron was to protect the airfield against the threat posed by German raiding parties landed by submarines and it was reinforced by 2822 Field Squadron in May 1944 when the threat of an attack on the airfield appeared more likely. Both squadrons returned to the UK in October 1944, for redeployment to 2TAF in NW Europe, and were replaced in the Azores by 2954 Field Squadron, which remained there until the war ended. Inevitably, the resident Regiment force was used to provide guards of honour for visiting British, American and Portuguese dignitaries in addition to its primary role of ground defence.

In ceremonial terms, however, the highlight of the war in general, and 1943 in particular, was the 25th Anniversary of the formation of the Royal Air Force, which was marked by granting the privilege of carrying out public duties in London to the Royal Air Force. Not surprisingly, the RAF Regiment was tasked to represent the RAF on this occasion and 2768 and 2773 Field Squadrons, commanded respectively by Squadron Leader AG Vaughan and Squadron Leader (later Group Captain) A. S. Cooper, mounted the guard at St James's and Buckingham Palaces. A number of distinguished RAF officers, including MRAF Lord Trenchard, the Father of the RAF, assembled in the forecourt of Buckingham Palace on the morning of 1 April 1943 to witness the blue-uniformed officers and airmen of the RAF Regiment taking over the sentry posts from the khaki-clad guardsmen of the Coldstream Guards.

Although the prospect of a successful return to the mainland of Europe may have seemed far away in mid-1943, preparations for that eventuality were already in progress and Wing Commander (later Group Captain) C. W. Mayhew of the RAF Regiment was the member

23

of the Allied Expeditionary Air Forces staff who was responsible for the detailed planning of the mobile defence of airfields following the invasion of France. The allocation of resources to the 2nd Tactical Air Force, which had been formed to operate with 21st Army Group in North West Europe after D-Day, included, with reserves, some sixty field and LAA squadrons of the RAF Regiment which were then withdrawn from airfields to begin their tactical training. There were no spare Regiment squadrons in the UK to replace them and officer and NCO instructors from other Regiment units were detached to train station personnel to defend their own stations against ground and air attack, an additional task which the RAF officers and airmen concerned did not particularly welcome.

Thus by the end of 1943 the RAF Regiment's manpower resources were stretched in every direction: squadrons were in action in the Mediterranean and Middle East as well as in the Far East where the arduous jungle campaign to recover Burma from the Japanese was beginning to take effect. The Regiment expeditionary force for Operation *Overlord* was in training for the forthcoming invasion of France and a large number of LAA squadrons remained deployed in south and east England for the defence of airfields from which aircraft were operating against targets in Europe, and from which the air effort for the invasion would be mounted. These continuing demands on the Regiment's limited resources were suddenly exacerbated by the Army's shortage of manpower and the resulting Prime Ministerial support for transfers of RAF airmen and RN ratings to fill the Army's depleted ranks.

From 1943 onwards the British Army had felt the effects of the casualties which it had sustained in the campaigns in Europe in 1940, in the Middle East in 1941, in the Far East in 1942 and in the Central Mediterranean in 1943. The infantry had, traditionally, born the brunt of these losses and the Guards regiments, in particular, had suffered more heavily than most. The preparations for the Second Front in Europe made it essential to bring the infantry battalions up to strength for the coming offensive and the War Office rebadged as many soldiers as it could find from its other arms and services to make good these deficiencies. Even this did not meet the manpower bill and in 1944 the RAF Regiment was ordered to transfer 2,000 NCOs and airmen to the Army, with another 5,000 following them in 1945, by disbanding many of the LAA squadrons which were deployed to defend RAF stations in the UK. The justification was the not unreasonable argument that the Luftwaffe no longer had the ability to attack targets in the UK, but an unexpected enemy response proved to be closer to hand than could have been imagined.

Renewed German air attack against the United Kingdom was to take the form of short-range unmanned flying bombs, the V1, powered by crude ram-jet engines and launched from northern France and the Low Countries against London and south-east England. These attacks began in June 1944, just as the Allied armies landed in Normandy, and despite air attacks on the launch sites and interceptions in flight by fighter aircraft, substantial numbers of 'doodlebugs' reached the Kent and Sussex coasts. Operation *Diver* involved the establishment of an anti-aircraft gun belt to counter this, and all available Royal Artillery and RAF Regiment anti-aircraft guns were redeployed in order to shoot down the V1s which had evaded the fighter screen. The western Diver gun belt was withdrawn in October 1944 as the advancing Allied armies in North-West Europe overran the launch sites which threatened that part of England but the eastern Diver belt remained operational to deal with further sporadic attacks until March 1945, by which time 21st Army Group's advance had driven the German launching sites out of range of southern England.

The sixty-eight RAF Regiment LAA squadrons which participated in Operation *Diver*, alongside LAA and HAA batteries of the Royal Artillery, contributed to the destruction of many of the V1s which had eluded the fighter screen over the English Channel. Although casualties were caused to Regiment personnel by V1 attacks on airfields occupied by British forces on the mainland of Europe, none were incurred by Regiment units in the UK from these weapons, which were programmed to overfly the gun belt in order to reach targets further inland.

The second weapon in the German *Vergeltungswaffen* arsenal was the V2, a true rocket, which, with its longer range, could be launched from sites which were still beyond the Allied front line in NW Europe. With ballistic trajectories and supersonic speed they were undetectable in flight and it was fortunate that they did not become operational until the closing months of the war. 2839 LAA Squadron had been withdrawn from the western Diver gun belt and redeployed with 2727 Squadron to Stapleford Tawney in Essex when, in January 1945, a V2 rocket hit the airfield. The explosion caused considerable damage to the buildings and installations on the RAF station, including the destruction of a 2839 Squadron lecture room in which one officer and ten NCOs and airmen were killed, and many more injured. The survivors were stunned by the pyschological effects of a devastating explosion occurring without prior warning, something which was to be experienced by the many Londoners who had to endure the results of V2 strikes on the metropolitan conurbation before the war ended.

As the build-up of forces for the return to Europe gathered

*A 40mm Bofors gun detachment, from one of the 68 RAF Regiment LAA squadrons which formed part of the Diver gun belt in SE England in 1944-45 to protect London from attack by V1 flying bombs.* (IWM-CH.13433)

momentum in 1943, Regiment field and LAA squadrons were constantly redeployed within the UK to practise them in the provision of mobile ground and LAA defence as aircraft moved from one airfield to another. Concurrently with training to meet this operational requirement, Regiment squadrons were rotated through the Combined Training Centres at Castle Toward, Dunoon and Inveraray where they were trained in landing craft embarkation techniques, amphibious landings and procedures within the beachhead. The training was concentrated, intensive, gruelling and competitive and squadrons were expected to carry out a demanding preparatory schedule to ensure that everyone received the maximum benefit from the CTC courses.

The commander of 2770 Field Squadron had a mock-up Landing Craft Tank constructed at RAF West Raynham to practise his men in the required embarkation and disembarkation procedures, loading and unloading drills, and amphibious assault techniques prior to attending the Inveraray course and strove to inspire them to greater efforts by conducting the training as inter-flight competitions. Officers and airmen entered into these exercises so enthusiastically that the training soon degenerated into open warfare within the squadron and had to be abandoned before serious injuries occurred. In order to cool everyone down (metaphorically, but not physically) the OC substituted a series of 25-mile route marches against the clock and squadron esprit-de-corps returned to normal. Not surprisingly, 2770 Squadron returned from CTC Inveraray with one of the highest gradings awarded to RAF units preparing for the forthcoming invasion.

The tempo increased in 1944 as preparations for the invasion of Europe moved towards finality. Within the Air Ministry the Directorate of Ground Defence had to contend with the disbanding of squadrons to meet reductions in global manning which had been imposed on the Regiment and the enforced transfer of Regiment NCOs and airmen, usually against their will, to the Army. At the same time, the staffs had to provide for thirty-eight (increasing to seventy-five by VE-Day) LAA, rifle and armoured car squadrons within 2TAF on the mainland of Europe, the formation of twenty-eight Wing HQs to control squadrons in the UK, the Mediterranean and Middle East, the Far East and North-West Europe and the reinforcement of Regiment units in the Far East as well as, despite dismissive comments from the Prime Minister himself, the retention of an air defence capability within the United Kingdom.

The launching of operational units into France under Operation *Overlord* on D-Day, and in the days which followed, was the largest task which the Regiment staffs faced during the war, but the landing and deployment of Regiment wings and squadrons in Normandy in June 1944 went according to plan. Thereafter the training, equipping and despatch of follow-up units and reinforcements became a priority as 2TAF and 21st Army Group advanced steadily towards Germany.

At the same time, wings and squadrons had to be earmarked for the Far East where the continuation of essential air support for General Slim's XIVth Army depended on the provision of RAF Regiment field and LAA squadrons to hold the forward airfields in the often fluid conditions of jungle warfare. Reinforcing units from the UK were assembled at Davidstowe Moor before embarking in troopships for the long, and usually uncomfortable, sea journey to Bombay, from where they had a lengthy rail journey across India to Secunderabad and Argatala before reaching Burma. To these problems were added the requirement to run down those LAA squadrons remaining in the UK and, by one means or another, transfer their NCOs and aircraftmen to the Army. From its peak of 240 squadrons in 1943, the Regiment was reduced to 188 squadrons in 1944 and to 100 by the end of 1945. The post-war run-down left only twenty-one squadrons in the RAF Regiment's order of battle by 1947.

# HOME DEFENCE UNITS 1942-1945

NOTE: Those units which were formed, and remained, in the United Kingdom throughout this period are listed below. Those which left the UK for service overseas are listed in the chapters covering the theatres in which they served.

## WING HEADQUARTERS
**1332** Bradwell Bay January 1945. Disbanded June 1945
**1333** Manston December 1944. Disbanded June 1945
**1334** Hawkinge January 1945. Disbanded June 1945
**1335** Kenley January 1945. Disbanded September 1945
**1337** Colerne January 1945. Disbanded September 1945
**1338** Detling January 1945. Disbanded October 1945

## SQUADRONS
**2702 LAA** – Harrow February 1942 – Yatesbury – *Diver* – Tangmere. No.2 Sqn October 1946
**2704 LAA** – Llanbedr February 1942 – Kenley – Tangmere – *Diver* – Disbanded October 1945
**2705 LAA** – Swansea February 1942 – Grantham – North Coates. Disbanded July 1944
**2707 LAA** – Ballykelly February 1942 – Gravesend – *Diver* – Lympne. Disbanded October 1945
**2709 LAA** – Henlow February 1942 – Detling – *Diver* – Hawkinge. Disbanded October 1945
**2711 LAA** – Crosby February 1942 – Bawdsey – Filey. Disbanded July 1944
**2712 LAA** – Ballyhalbert February 1942 – Mildenhall – Lakenheath. Disbanded July 1944
**2714 LAA** – Wormwell February 1942 – Skeabrae. Awards: 1 MID. Disbanded July 1944
**2716 LAA** – Finningley February 1942 – Skitten – Holme. Disbanded July 1944
**2718 LAA** – Leeming February 1942 – Hornchurch – Ford. Disbanded June 1945

**2720 LAA** – Linton-on-Ouse February 1942 – Manston – *Diver*. Disbanded September 1945

**2722 LAA** – Newton February 1942 – Folkestone – *Diver*. Disbanded February 1945

**2723 LAA** – Oakington February 1942 – Tangmere – North Weald. Disbanded September 1945

**2725 LAA** – Stradishall February 1942 – Swingate. Disbanded April 1944

**2727 LAA** – Syerston February 1942 – Eastbourne- *Diver*. Awards: 1 BEM+2 MID. Disbanded February 1946

**2728 LAA** – Waterbeach February 1942 – Swingate – Branscombe. Disbanded June 1944

**2730 LAA** – Wyton February 1942 – Bawdsey – Grantham. Depot Sqn June 1944

**2732 LAA** – Bassingbourne February 1942 – Rye – *Diver*. Disbanded April 1945

**2733 LAA** – Benson February 1942 – Hawkinge – *Diver*. Disbanded April 1945

**2735 LAA** – Bramcote February 1942 – Allhallows – *Diver*. Disbanded April 1945

**2745 LAA** – Leuchars February 1942 – Biggin Hill-Isle of White. Disbanded October 1943

**2746 LAA** – Lossiemouth February 1942 – Detling – *Diver*. Awards: 1 MID. Disbanded September 1944

**2747 LAA** – Kinloss February 1942 – Filey. Disbanded October 1945

**2751 LAA** – Sullom Voe February 1942 – Eastchurch. Disbanded July 1944

**2752 LAA** – Stranraer February 1942 – Swingate – Hawkshill Down. Disbanded April 1945

**2753 LAA** – Turnhouse February 1942 – Allhallows – *Diver*. Disbanded November 1945

**2754 LAA** – Limavady February 1942 – Stradishall. Disbanded July 1944

**2755 LAA** – Maghaberry February 1942 – West Raynham. Disbanded July 1944

**2756 LAA** – Eglinton February 1942 – Coningsby. Disbanded July 1944

**2758 LAA** – Aberporth February 1942 – Foulness – *Diver*. Disbanded June 1945

**2761 LAA** – Bottisham February 1942 – Southend – *Diver*. Disbanded April 1945

**2762 LAA** – Cardiff February 1942 – Beaulieu – Manston. Disbanded July 1945

**2763 LAA** – Doncaster February 1942 – Lympne – Wyton.
Disbanded August 1945

**2764 Field** – Perton February 1942 – LAA May 1943 – Disbanded
June 1943

**2766 LAA** – Kidsale February 1942 – Brookland – *Diver*. Disbanded
Oct 1945

**2767 LAA** – Manorbier February 1942 -Hastings – *Diver*.
Awards: 1 MID. Disbanded October 1945

**2769 LAA** – Old Sarum February 1942-West Malling- *Diver*.
Awards: 1 BEM. Disbanded October 1945

**2772 LAA** – Towyn February 1942 – Warmwell. Disbanded April
1945

**2774 LAA** – Longkesh February 1942 – St Leonards – *Diver*.
Disbanded April 1945

**2775 LAA** – Newtownards February 1942 – Middle Wallop.
Disbanded October 1943

**2776 LAA** – Helensburgh February 1942 – Swinderby. Rifle October
1944. Disbanded February 1945

**2778 LAA** – Jurby February 1942 – Maidstone – *Diver*. Disbanded
May 1945

**2779 LAA** – Netheravon February 1942 – Helston. Disbanded April
1945

**2780 LAA** – Penrhos February 1942 – Smiths Lawn. Disbanded
April 1945

**2782 LAA** – Manby February 1942 – St Eval. Disbanded July 1945

**2783 LAA** – Upavon February 1942 – Swingate. Disbanded July 1945

**2784 LAA** – West Freugh February 1942 – Dyce. Rifle October
1944. Disbanded  February 1945

**2785 LAA** – Chivenor February 1942. Disbanded July 1944

**2787 LAA** – Chester February 1942 – Martlesham Heath.
Disbanded April 1945

**2789 LAA** – Montrose February 1942 – Tangmere. Disbanded
October 1944

**2790 LAA** – Worcester February 1942 – Merston – *Diver*. Disbanded
October 1944

**2792 LAA** – Kidlington February 1942 – Friston – *Diver*. Disbanded
April 1945

**2793 LAA** – Grantham February 1942 – Detling – *Diver*. Disbanded
April 1945

**2795 LAA** – Bovingdon February 1942 – Foulness – *Diver*.
Disbanded October 1945

**2796 LAA** – Ronaldsway February 1942 – Allhallows – *Diver*.
Awards 2 BEM.  Disbanded April 1945

**2797 LAA** – North Luffenham February 1942 – Littlestone – *Diver*. Disbanded April 1945

**2799 LAA** – Grangemouth February 1942 – Hawkinge – *Diver*. Disbanded October 1945

**2801 LAA** – Northolt February 1942 – Isle of Wight. Disbanded April 1945

**2803 LAA** – Sealand February 1942 – Friston – *Diver*. Disbanded October 1945

**2808 LAA** – Polebrook February 1942 – Kingston. Disbanded October 1944

**2813 LAA** – Thurleigh February 1942 – Merston – *Diver*. Awards: 1 MID. Disbanded June 1945

**2815 LAA** – Atcham February 1942 – Merryfield. Disbanded October 1944

**2818 LAA** – Theale February 1942 – Folkestone – *Diver*. Disbanded April 1945

**2820 LAA** – Atcham February 1942 – Southend – *Diver*. Awards: 1 BEM+1 MID. Disbanded May 1945

**2821 LAA** – Perth February 1942 – Thorney Island. Disbanded October 1945

**2828 LAA** – Honeybourne February 1942 – Detling – *Diver*. Disbanded August 1945

**2832 LAA** – Honiley February 1942 – Shoreham – Tangmere. Disbanded April 1945

**2833 LAA** – Hadley February 1942 – Driffield. Disbanded July 1944

**2835 LAA** – Woodvale February 1942 – Hooe – *Diver*. Disbanded April 1945

**2836 LAA** – St Angelo February 1942 – Swanton Morley. Disbanded July 1944

**2839 LAA** – Marston Moor February 1942 – Southend – *Diver*. Disbanded August 1945

**2840 LAA** – Ossington February 1942 – Bradwell Bay – *Diver*. Disbanded August 1945

**2841 LAA** – Benbecula February 1942 – High Wycombe. Disbanded February 1945

**2842 LAA** – Tiree February 1942 – Binbrook. Awards: 1 MID. Disbanded July 1944

**2849 LAA** – Wing February 1942 – Shoreham. Depot Sqn June 1944

**2850 LAA** – Aldergrove February 1942 – St Athan. Disbanded November 1943

**2851 LAA** – Maydown February 1942 – Tarrant Rushton. Disbanded November 1943

**2860 LAA** – Leuchars February 1942. Disbanded September 1942

**2877 LAA** – Kingscliffe June 1943 – Southend – *Diver*.
Disbanded October 1944

**2882 LAA** – Kingscliffe June 1943 – Folkestone – *Diver*.
Disbanded April 1945

**2884 LAA** – Bedford June 1943 – Eastchurch.
Disbanded November 1943

**2885 LAA** – Zeals June 1943 – Coltishall. Disbanded October 1943

**2886 LAA** – Riccall – June 1943 – Hawkinge – *Diver*.
Disbanded April 1945

**2887 LAA** – Castle Camps June 1943 – Wick. Disbanded October 1943

**2888 LAA** – Christchurch June 1943 – Ibsley – Odiham.
Disbanded October 1943

**2889 LAA** – Fairlop June 1943 – Lydd – *Diver*. Disbanded May 1945

**2890 LAA** – Waddington June 1943 – Rye – *Diver*.
Disbanded April 1945

**2891 LAA** – Dartmouth June 1943 – Lydd – *Dive*r.
Disbanded April 1945

**2892 LAA** – Exmouth July 1943 – Rye – *Diver*. Disbanded April 1945

**2893 LAA** – Ludham October 1942 – Bognor – *Diver*.
Disbanded October 1944

**2894 LAA** – Tangmere June 1943 – Rye – *Diver*. Disbanded June 1945

**2895 LAA** – Hastings June 1943 – Gatwick – *Diver*.
Disbanded October 1943

**2899 LAA** – North Luffenham June 1943 – North Coates.
Disbanded  October 1943

**2947 LAA** – Longcross June 1943 – Filey – Sennen.
Disbanded March 1945

**2948 LAA** – Ventnor Febrary 1944 – Swingate. Disbanded April 1945

**2950 LAA** – Longcross July 1943 – Brandy Bay. Disbanded March 1945

**2951 LAA** – Trueleigh Hill August 1943 – Rye. Disbanded March 1945

**2952 LAA** – North Luffenham August 1943 – Netheravon.
Disbanded October 1943

**2953 LAA** – Wellingore June 1943 – Bolt Head.
Disbanded October 1943

**2954 LAA** – Driffield June 1943 – Leuchars – Azores – UK.
Disbanded September 1945

**2955 LAA** – St Athan June 1943 – Hawkinge. Disbanded April 1945

**2956 LAA** – Waddington June 1943 – Merston.
Disbanded November  1943

**2957 LAA** – Locking July 1943 – Waterbeach. Depot Sqn June 1944

# CHAPTER FOUR

# NORTH AFRICA 1942-43

In 1942 the British and Americans were under pressure from the Russians to mount a second front in Europe to draw German forces away from the eastern front. However, the abortive raid on Dieppe in August of that year had revealed how much more would have to be done before the Allied armies could invade Europe with any assurance of success. At that time France was still divided into two parts – the north and west occupied by the Germans and the south and east under the control of a puppet French government at Vichy, headed by Marshal Pétain. Vichy France continued to exercise control over French possessions in North Africa and this provided the Allies with an opportunity to exploit divisions within occupied France for the benefit of the growing number of supporters of the anti-German resistance movements within occupied Europe. Plans were accordingly drawn up for a joint Anglo-American invasion of North Africa, codenamed Operation *Torch*, in November 1942, which would not only complete the defeat of the Axis forces which were retreating from Alamein to Tunis but also develop the techniques of a landing on enemy territory by Allied forces at a distance from the main base.

Headquarters No.333 Group was established in offices in St James's Square in London to plan the RAF's participation in Operation *Torch*. Among the assembled staff officers was Lieutenant-Colonel H. M. Salmon MC, who had been posted from Headquarters Coastal Command as the designated senior RAF Regiment officer in the Group, which would become Eastern Air Command of the Allied Forces North Africa when the invasion took place later that year.

Morrey Salmon was an inspired choice to lead the RAF Regiment in its first campaign of the war. Although not a regular officer – he had left the Army in 1919 – he was a successful company director with wide experience in restructuring organizations and dealing with people from every walk of life. Although small in stature, he was a big man in every other sense and his strong personality, coupled with his determination to lead the RAF Regiment to success, was to ensure that he was able to introduce a series of innovations and reorganizations which enabled his units to make their unique contribution to air operations in North Africa and the Central Mediterranean theatres.

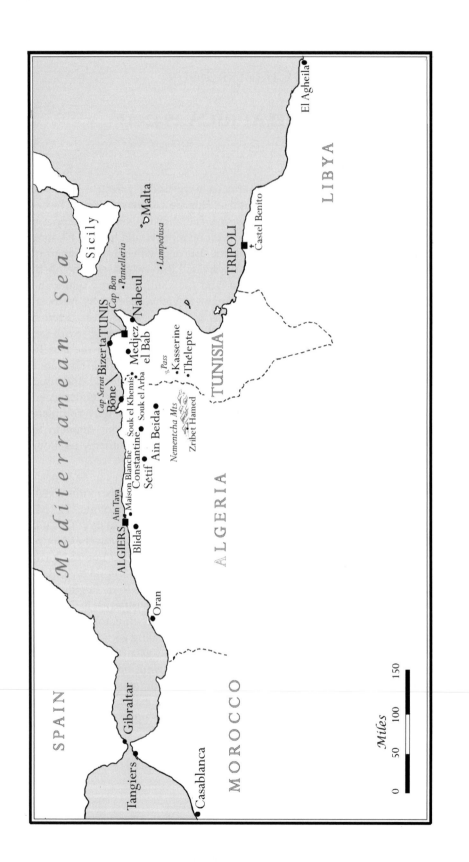

SPAIN

Gibraltar

Tangiers

Casablanca

MOROCCO

Oran

ALGIERS

Ain Taya

Maison Blanche

Blida

Sétif

Constantine

Souk el Khemis

Souk el Arba

Ain Beida

Nementcha Mts

Zribet Hamed

ALGERIA

Mediterranean Sea

Cap Serrat

Bizerta

Bône

Cap Bon

TUNIS

Medjez
el Bab

Nabeul

Pantelleria

Pass

Kasserine

Thélepte

TUNISIA

Sicily

Malta

Lampedusa

TRIPOLI

Castel Benito

LIBYA

El Agheila

Miles

0    50    100    150

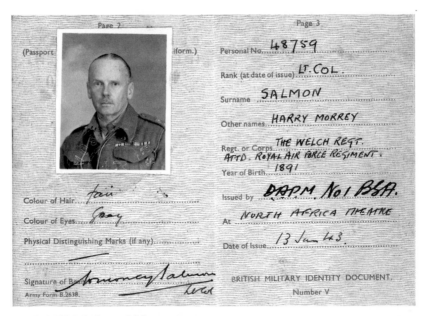

(Passport                                    iform.)        Personal No. 48759

                                                            Rank (at date of issue) LT.COL.

                                                            Surname  SALMON

                                                            Other names  HARRY MORREY

                                                            Regt. or Corps  THE WELCH REGT.
                                                            ATTD. ROYAL AIR FORCE REGIMENT.
                                                            Year of Birth  1891

Colour of Hair. fair                                        Issued by  DAPM No1 BSA.

Colour of Eyes. gray                                        At  NORTH AFRICA THEATRE

Physical Distinguishing Marks (if any)                      Date of Issue  13 Jan 43.

Signature of Bearer                                         BRITISH MILITARY IDENTITY DOCUMENT.
Army Form B.2638.                                           Number V

*Lt Col HM Salmon MC.* (N. Salmon)

The RAF transit camp at West Kirby in Lancashire was an unprepossessing starting point for almost three thousand officers and men of the RAF Regiment who assembled there in October 1942 to form the ground and air defence contingent for the six aircraft wings in the invasion force. There were five field squadrons, totalling some 850 all ranks, a further 300 officers and airmen in five independent anti-aircraft flights, and an additional 1,600 RAF Regiment personnel who were distributed among the other RAF units in order to provide them with integral ground and anti-aircraft defence resources. In the event, this concept of using specialist personnel in such ineffectual groupings did not survive the test of war and even before the North African campaign had ended these officers and men were withdrawn from a variety of tasks in the rear areas and reorganized into RAF Regiment squadrons and flights to make a more effective contribution to air operations in the combat zone.

Embarking their passengers in Liverpool, the troop transports sailed to the concentration area in the Clyde and on a grey October day in 1942 the first of the six convoys, which eventually totalled over 600 merchant vessels and escorting Royal Navy warships, sailed for the Straits of Gibraltar and the North African coast. Thanks to a comprehensive deception plan, which resulted in the U-boat packs being deployed on the approaches to West Africa, and to the German preoccupation with events in the Western Desert following the Battle of

*Personnel of Nos. 4088 and 4089 AA Flights scrambling down the side of a troopship off the Algerian coast prior to landing on the beaches at Ain Taya on 8th November 1942.*
(IWM-CNA.28)

Alamein, the leading British convoy, KM.1, reached Ain Taya, east of Algiers, without incident and landed its assault forces on the windswept beaches on a cold and overcast November day. Unfortunately, the deteriorating sea state prevented the vehicles and equipment of Nos. 4088 and 4089 AA Flights RAF Regiment from joining the officers and airmen who were already on the shore. Within 24 hours, however, Algiers harbour had been captured and the remaining elements of the two AA flights were landed on the dockside and reunited with those personnel who had come ashore on the previous day.

Although the landings at Casablanca, Oran and Algiers were unopposed, when the British and Americans armies advanced inland they met strong resistance from some of the French garrisons, which were supported by German and Italian aircraft operating from Tunisian airfields. The port installations at Algiers had been damaged in this fighting and the harbour proved too small to cope with the mass of men and equipment which were landed. Not only was materiel dumped on the dockside without regard to its ultimate forward destination, but units and their stores had been loaded in separate ships in the UK and often arrived days apart. Consequently, time spent in locating vehicles, weapons and equipment inevitably delayed the deployment of operational units to the combat zone. It was, however, a useful lesson in how not to conduct the logistic support for an invasion and one which paid dividends in terms of improved planning and organization for subsequent amphibious landings, especially the invasion of France in June 1944.

Meanwhile, the RAF aircraft which had flown into the former French airfields at Maison Blanche and Bône were already under air attack by the Luftwaffe and the Regia Aeronautica – and even by some French aircraft. The arrival of 4088 Flight at Maison Blanche and of 4089 at Bône went some way towards redressing the balance and the anti-aircraft fire from their guns shot down several of the attackers as well as deterring others from pressing home their attacks. Nevertheless, the weight of the enemy air attack caused both damage and casualties on the airfields. At Bône Flight Lieutenant Law, Sergeant Hersnip, Corporal Barker and LACs Morris and Paterson of 4089 Flight were killed when air attacks were directed at gun positions and similar enemy action at Canrobert killed Corporal Harved and wounded other members of a 4090 Flight gun detachment.

The arrival of the follow-up convoys KM.2 and KM.3 were welcome in that they brought Lieutenant-Colonel Salmon, the five field squadrons and the remaining three AA flights, but the congestion in the port was such that these units had great difficulty in getting ashore and locating their unit equipment. The liner *Scythia*, with 2788 Field

Squadron embarked, was torpedoed off Algiers but remained afloat and was able to dock in the port. Nevertheless, it was several days before the disembarking units could locate their vehicles and equipment and move to their assigned operational locations.

The RAF component of the invasion force consisted of six wings of aircraft – four fighter, one light bomber and one general reconnaissance – deployed on six main bases and three forward airfields. With only five field squadrons and five AA flights available, priority for defence was given to the one light bomber and four fighter wings. The initial deployment was 2788 Field Squadron and 4089 AA Flight at La Calle airfield (Bône) with 322 Fighter Wing, 2825 Field Squadron and 4088 AA Flight at Maison Blanche with 323 Fighter Wing, 2744 Field Squadron and 4091 AA Flight at Constantine with 324 Fighter Wing, while 2721 Field Squadron and 4092 AA Flight waited for the aircraft of 325 Fighter Wing to arrive before being assigned to a forward airfield. The light bombers of 326 Wing were at Setif and Ain Beida with 2771 Field Squadron and 4090 AA Flight; the aircraft of 328 General Reconnaissance Wing were at the undefended airfield at Blida, which was far enough from the front line to be considered less likely to suffer the attention of the enemy air force. Early in December it was found necessary to move 324 Wing to a new airfield further forward to improve the air cover over the forward positions of 1st Army. 2825 Field Squadron and 4088 AA Flight were accordingly redeployed from Maison Blanche to the new advanced airfield at Souk el Arba.

Convoy KM.5, with the rear echelons of the field squadrons embarked, was 70 miles from Algiers when it was intercepted by a U-boat. The troop transport P 15 (the former passenger liner *Strathallan*) was hit by a torpedo at about 0215hrs on 21 December and began to settle in the water. While the other troops on board took to the boats and life rafts and cast off from what was thought to be a sinking ship, the senior RAF Regiment officer ordered the Regiment contingent to stand fast and remain on board. During this confused situation Pilot Officer Dodd of 2788 Squadron and LAC Turner of 2825 Squadron unhesitatingly dived from the ship into the dark, oily waters to rescue an Army officer and a soldier who had fallen into the sea while attempting to board a lifeboat. Wing Commander R. G. Seymour, the OC troops on board *Strathallan*, subsequently reported that the steadfast behaviour of the Regiment officers and airmen had set a magnificent example to everyone else on board.

Although the selfless actions of Dodd and Turner were subsequently recognized by the award of the MBE and the BEM respectively, it later became clear that the RAF's administrative system had difficulty in appreciating the significance of citations for gallantry in action against the enemy by RAF Regiment personnel. There were to be many examples, later in the campaign, of recommendations being downgraded or rejected by RAF headquarters, either because of unfamiliarity with the conditions of fighting in a ground or air defence environment, or by a reluctance to encroach on the Army's monopoly of such awards for military operations.

*Strathallan* did not sink as rapidly as those who abandoned her had feared and she was still afloat but well down in the water when, at 1100 hrs on 22 December, the destroyer HMS *Panther* came alongside the stricken vessel, took off the RAF Regiment personnel and landed them at Oran. Inevitably, all their weapons, equipment and personal kit were lost with *Strathallan* and they arrived at Algiers on board the troop transports *Duchess of Richmond* and *Duchess of York* with only the clothes they were wearing. Lieutenant-Colonel Salmon then exploited his Army connections and prevailed on the 1st Army's RAOC staff officers to replace the lost weapons, unit and personal equipment for the Regiment officers and airmen as a matter of urgency.

With his entire force now operational in North Africa, Morrey Salmon approached the Air Officer Commanding with a radical proposal. This was that the Regiment units should no longer be considered as part of the support element on RAF airfields, where they were controlled by the senior administrative officer, but instead should form part of the operational element of flying squadrons and wings under the direct control of the station commander. This was readily agreed, with the result that from then onwards the Regiment squadrons were employed in a flexible and aggressive role, occupying and defending forward airfields in accordance with the RAF's requirements, rather than having to depend on the availability, or otherwise, of Army units for such tasks. This gave the Air Commander greater flexibility in deploying his aircraft to the most suitable locations for operations against the enemy in the knowledge that these would be protected by Regiment units under his control. Accordingly, by late November all ten RAF Regiment units were deployed on forward airfields.

In January 1943 2744 Field Squadron and 4091 AA Flight advanced from Constantine to join 2825 Field Squadron and 4088 AA Flight near Souk el Khemis where three new landing grounds (Euston, Waterloo and Paddington) had been constructed. Here the ever-present threat of air attack had been increased by the warning of parachute or glider-borne assaults on one or more of these forward airfields. Shortly afterwards another airfield (Tingley) was built on the eastern edge of Lac Fetzara, to the west of Bône, and 2788 Field Squadron and 4089 AA Flight moved from La Calle to provide its defence. The momentum of the advance eastwards continued with the deployment of 2771 Field Squadron and 4090 AA Flight from Canrobert to Oulmene, where they occupied a new satellite airstrip before making the difficult journey across the Nementcha Mountains to Zribet Hamed to establish an emergency landing ground for night operations during the period of the full moon.

Meanwhile Group Captain David Atcherley, commanding 325 (Night Fighter) Wing, was concerned that the nightly stream of enemy transport aircraft carrying supplies to the Afrika Korps from Sicily and Italy was not being intercepted by his fighter aircraft. His problem was the lack of ground radars to direct the RAF aircraft – and his solution was to deploy ground control interception units on the Tunisian coast. The ideal location was at Cap Serrat, where a lighthouse was held by a small Royal Navy detachment, on the undefended left flank of 1st Army's forward positions. The Army's view was that the best part of an infantry battalion would be necessary to secure and hold the Cap Serrat area – but this could not be provided by the overstretched 139 Brigade whose northernmost positions were a good ten miles south of Cap Serrat. In view of the importance of this task, 2721 Field Squadron and 4092 AA Flight were tasked with escorting the radar units which, for security purposes, were designated "Air Ministry Experimental Stations" (in this case Nos 8009 and 8010 AMES) to Cap Serrat and protecting them while they carried out the vital task of directing night fighters onto unsuspecting German and Italian transport aircraft.

The Regiment units moved out of Setif on 29 January to rendezvous with the AMES at Tabarka, from where the convoy moved on the Tunis road to Tamera and Sedjenane, At that point the route degenerated into a rough track through broken country for the last 20 miles to Cap Serrat and the difficulties of moving the heavy radar vehicles were such that it was not until 6 February that the AMES were completely operational in their new location. As the enemy had almost complete air superiority in the area, the convoy was subjected to frequent air attacks, which damaged vehicles and caused casualties to personnel, during the journey. On the other hand, the vehicle-mounted Browning guns of 4092 Flight accounted for several of the low-flying Fw190s which attacked the column during its slow journey. By the time the column reached Cap Serrat the weather had made the track completely impassable for vehicles, but Pilot Officer Steele of 2721 Squadron used his initiative to form an animal transport column by hiring camels and donkeys from the local Arabs for the resupply of the Cap Serrat garrison.. He then controlled the loading and movements of these supply trains on their journeys from the roadhead at Sedjenane over difficult terrain to the coast.

Given the intensity of enemy air activity in that area, the decision was made to conceal the occupation of Cap Serrat from the air by refraining from any hostile actions – not an easy task for the anti-aircraft gunners who had to hold their fire when Me109s and Fw190s circled the lighthouse and used it for target practice. This self-restraint was successful in that the enemy did not appreciate that the night fighters which were destroying Axis transport aircraft on the Sicily-Tunisia route every night owed their success to RAF radars concealed at Cap Serrat. As the month of February progressed, Lieutenant-Colonel Salmon became concerned at the increasing enemy activity in the area to the east of Cap Serrat and deployed the newly-formed 4352 AA Flight as a rifle flight to reinforce the defences of the radar units.

Towards the end of February 1943 2788 Field Squadron and 4089 AA Flight were ordered to move to Cap Serrat to take over from 2721 Squadron and 4092 Flight. This deployment was fortuitous as on 26 February the German army launched a strong attack towards Cap Serrat and drove back the outposts of the Corps Franc d'Afrique which were screening the left flank of the British line. On the following day, when the enemy's patrols were observed on the coastal hills only three miles from Cap Serrat, 139 Brigade began to withdraw to avoid being outflanked and exposed the RAF positions to the advancing enemy. On advice from the brigade commander, Group Captain Atcherley decided to evacuate Cap Serrat and ordered that any vehicles and equipment which could not be moved were to be destroyed. The Royal Navy was able to load the AMES vehicles and stores onto small craft on 28 February and the remaining vehicles and personnel were ordered to leave the Cap without delay. It was a difficult operation, carried out over rough tracks with the close support of 2721 Squadron and 4092 AA Flight while 2788 Squadron and 4089 Flight formed the rearguard which held off the forward elements of the advancing enemy. Once the main column had reached safety, 2788 Squadron was placed under command of 139 Brigade, holding part of the line with a battalion of the Corps Franc d'Afrique, until the German drive had been checked and the British brigade was able to reoccupy its former positions.

It was at this time that the Commander RAF Regiment had successfully completed negotiations with his Army counterparts for heavier support weapons for his five field squadrons. The field batteries of the Royal Artillery in the theatre had just received new 25 pounder field guns to replace the modified 18 pounder field guns of an earlier vintage which had been upgraded to fire 25 pounder ammunition. A number of the 18/25 pounder guns were held surplus to Army requirements in the ordnance field park at Algiers and twenty of these useful artillery pieces – four per field squadron – were loaned to the RAF Regiment. After a short period of training by Royal Artillery NCOs, these guns, with their ability to fire both high explosive and anti-tank rounds, became invaluable support weapons for the field squadrons in the fluid conditions of warfare which were a feature of the remainder of the North African campaign.

Further south, the German army, fighting a rearguard action against the advancing 8th Army in the east, launched a fierce attack on the inexperienced American divisions which were holding the line of the Tunisian-Algerian border to the west. The battle-hardened Afrika Korps brushed the American defences aside and had seized the key area of the Kasserine Pass by 20 February. Aircraft of 326 (Light Bomber) Wing had been deployed to the forward landing ground at Zribet Hamed, which was now threatened by the sudden German advance, and the group captain commanding the wing was ordered to withdraw his aircraft, ground crews and vehicles to a more secure airfield in Tunisia. Group Captain Laurence Sinclair was, however, made of sterner stuff and, having ordered his aircraft to fly out, moved his servicing personnel and RAF Regiment units to a defensive position on the high ground which he planned to hold in order to deny the use of the airfield to the advancing German columns. Squadron Leader Willington's 2771 Squadron, with its field artillery and armoured cars, and the anti-aircraft guns of 4090 Flight, formed the core of the Zribet Hamed strongpoint, but to the disappointment of 'Sinclairforce' the British 1st Army's counter-attack recaptured the lost ground and drove the Germans back into Tunisia before they could reach the RAF's forward landing grounds.

As the campaign developed, Lieutenant-Colonel Salmon had advanced his plans for making more effective use of the forty-two officers and 1600 NCOs and aircraftmen of the RAF Regiment who were scattered in small groups throughout the remainder of the Eastern Air Command. In theory, these airmen were established to provide the specialized ground and anti-aircraft defence element in the supporting units; in fact, they were being misused as batmen for senior officers and fatigue parties for station warrant officers to the extent that they were quite ineffective in their primary role. By obtaining General Liardet's approval for his plans in the first instance, he was able to secure his AOC's ready agreement to the reorganization of these manpower resources into 24 additional AA Flights, which were numbered from 4337 to 4360, early in February 1943. The formation of these new flights was carried out so rapidly that it was some time before Air Ministry realized that the block of numbers which had been allocated to North Africa overlapped with AA flight numbers which were already in use in Air Command South-East Asia and an urgent instruction went out from London to Delhi in May 1943 to renumber the AA flights in India and Burma in the series 4401-4450 to avoid any further confusion in the overall order of battle.

As the direct enemy threat to the RAF's airfields receded, Lieutenant-Colonel Salmon took steps to employ his squadrons in an active role by detaching them in turn to forward Army formations. 2788 Field Squadron was the first to be attached to 38th Infantry Brigade in March 1943 when they took over a sector south of the road Testour-Medjez el Bab from the London Irish. The squadron's armoured car flight was attached to 56th Reconnaissance Regiment Royal Armoured Corps and patrolled into the no-man's-land along the road Medjez el Bab-Oued Zarga and into the Goubellat plain. The support flight, with its 25 pounder field guns, joined 67th Field Regiment Royal Artillery and participated in their fire tasks on various enemy targets.

In April 2744 Field Squadron, with 4091 AA Flight under command, was attached to 24th Guards Brigade and took over a sector with a frontage of 5,000 yards on the hills south of, and overlooking, the road Medjez el Bab-Oued Zarga from 5th Northants on the left of 1st Irish Guards. The armoured car flight was attached to the 1st Divisional Reconnaissance Regiment and carried out a number of patrols, during which one of the flight's armoured cars received a direct hit from an enemy anti-tank gun. One crew member was wounded, but was extricated from the wrecked vehicle by another crewman, AC1 Robert Quigley, who dismounted a Bren LMG from the disabled vehicle and engaged the enemy until all his ammunition had been expended. He then helped his wounded comrade into the cover of broken ground and both evaded the enemy who were searching for them. 24 hours later Quigley reached the British lines with the wounded airman and returned to his unit.

The squadron's support flight was attached to an artillery regiment south of Testour and participated in the fire plan which harassed the German positions by day and night. With 248 Field Company Royal Engineers under command, the squadron cleared minefields and secured the start line for a battalion group attack on the enemy-held hills to the north of the road. Following this successful attack, 2774 Squadron advanced into Medjez el Bab and became responsible for the defence of the northern approaches to the town.

Within a few days 2721 Field Squadron, with 4092 AA Flight under command, also arrived in the front line and was deployed to the east of Medjez el Bab, under command of 3rd Infantry Brigade. The squadron was assigned to a position in the Belle Farm locality facing the German stronghold of Grich el Oued and holding the sector between 5th

Grenadier Guards and 2744 Squadron. On the night of 20/21 April a German counter-attack was launched on Medjez el Bab salient and enemy armour was engaged at close range by the 25 pounder guns of 2721 Squadron's support flight. In this battle one airmen was killed and several others wounded by fire from the enemy's Mark IV tanks before they were disabled or driven off by the intensity of the British defensive fire.

In the following days the Regiment positions were under constant artillery and air attack but the Browning machine guns of 4092 AA Flight reduced the effectiveness of the enemy aircraft by accounting for several of the attacking fighters and bombers. Patrols from 2721 Squadron and 4092 Flight were active in no-man's-land where they captured several reconnaissance parties of Italian paratroops as well as rescuing the crews of a number of RAF and USAAF aircraft which had been brought down in the desert beyond the British lines and recovering vital equipment from the crashed aircraft before it could fall into enemy hands.

On 3 May 2721 Squadron was transferred to 2nd Infantry Brigade and occupied the ridge east of Point 145, forward of 1st Reconnaissance Regiment's positions and overlooking the Krenoub Gap on the right boundary of 1st (British) division. The Germans launched an attack on the Gab-Gab Gap on the following morning and brought heavy mortar and artillery fire down on Point 145 and the adjoining ridge. The attack was held and the counter-attack that evening seized the hill feature of Djebel Bou Aoukaz, enabling a full-scale offensive by XI Corps to be launched the next day.

Meanwhile 2771 Field Squadron remained at Canrobert, with elements detached to forward landing grounds at Ouleme and Thelepte where the deputy squadron commander, Flight Lieutenant Fleming,

*2721 Sqn 25pdr field gun in anti-tank role at Medjez-el-Bab, 1943* (HM Salmon)

was killed when his jeep was hit and overturned during an attack. More parachute troops had been infiltrated to reconnoitre the airfields but patrols from the squadron searched the surrounding hills and brought back Italian and German parachutists whom they had captured, sometimes after brisk exchanges of fire.

As the advance of the 1st Army from the west and 8th Army from the east squeezed the Axis forces into the coastal area between Bizerta and Tunis, from which there was no escape for them, plans were formulated to seize headquarters, aircraft and technical equipment before they could be destroyed by the enemy or looted by the forward units of 1st and 8th Armies. "S" Force was formed from groups of specialist personnel to enter Bizerta, Tunis and Nabeul ahead of the main bodies of the British and American armies and secure designated items of enemy equipment and personnel. The nominated personnel of "S" Force included intelligence and psyops teams, fuel, weapons and technical specialists drawn from all three British services as well as representatives of the civil and military government departments and the American and French forces. This impressive, but motley, collection of experts did not have a combatant capability and so the escort and strike elements of "S" Force were provided by three field squadrons (2721, 2744 and 2788) and three AA flights (4089, 4091 and 4337) of the RAF Regiment.

Assembling at Ain Tounga on 6/7 May, "S" Force moved off in three groups and reached their objectives the following day. The Regiment units were the first British troops to enter Ferryville and were close behind the leading British armour into Bizerta and Tunis, where they encountered spasmodic resistance from some German units, which was soon overcome. Airfields and key points were secured and over 3,000 prisoners taken by the Regiment units, leaving the "S" Force specialist teams free to pursue their tasks until the force was disbanded on 12 May.

2788 Squadron and 4337 Flight were then ordered to clear the Cap Bon peninsula of the remaining pockets of enemy resistance. Here more determined resistance was encountered but the speed and firepower of the Regiment force overcame the opposition and within 24 hours all the remaining enemy personnel had laid down their arms and surrendered. The armoured car flight of 2788 Squadron, commanded by Flying Officer Thomas Dun, advanced rapidly into the Cap Bon peninsula to seize the landing ground at Korbous. Despite the hostile enemy reaction, the airfield was captured before the serviceable aircraft there could be destroyed and a large number of Luftwaffe officers and men were taken prisoner.

A follow-up operation into the surrounding hills by 4337 AA Flight, under the command of Flight Lieutenant Arthur Langham, encountered more German resistance at a field headquarters and supply dump but a spirited attack by Langham and his men captured the enemy position and its garrison of 200 German soldiers. After regrouping his flight, he sent patrols out into the neighbouring hills to locate a further 900 enemy personnel who were trying to evade capture. Corporal Thomas Boyd was a patrol commander who distinguished himself by leading his men in a skirmish with an enemy platoon and after a short fire fight, took twenty-five prisoners. Leaving his patrol to guard the prisoners, Corporal Boyd set out alone to reconnoitre another enemy position and single-handedly forced the surrender of a complete machine-gun section.

Having cleared the Cap Bon peninsula of the enemy, 2788 Squadron and 4337 Flight were on the road back to Tunis when they met the leading tanks of the 8th Army's vanguard coming towards them and Flight Lieutenant Langham was somewhat concerned that the approaching British armour might mistake them for the Luftwaffe's ground troops. Fortunately, the Army recognized the RAF Regiment column and greeted them in a friendly manner as they headed into the area in which the Regiment had already brought German resistance to an end.

The North African campaign officially ended on 13 May 1943 with Field Marshal Alexander's dispatch to the Prime Minister: "Sir, it is my duty to report that the Tunisian campaign is over. All enemy resistance has ceased. We are masters of the North African shores." Officers and men drawn from all the RAF Regiment units in the theatre took part in the victory parade in Tunis on 20 May 1943. By the end of the campaign, the Army had reclaimed the 25 pounder field guns which had been loaned to the RAF Regiment squadrons, but generously replaced them with a one-for-one issue of anti-tank guns.

The final honours list for the North African campaign included the OBE for Wing Commander E. M. Downes, MCs for Flight Lieutenant A. C. Langham of 4337 Flight and Flying Officer T Dun of 2788 Squadron and MMs for Corporal J. Boyd of 4337 Flight and AC1 R Quigley of 2744 Squadron. Lieutenant-Colonel H. M. Salmon, Squadron Leader Fleming-Smith of 2825 Squadron, Flight Lieutenant Cely-Trevilian and LAC Eaton of 2721 Squadron, Flying Officer Richardson, Sergeant Lumsden, Corporal Bolt, Corporal Fisher and LAC Youngs of 2744 Squadron, Warrant Officer Lovell of 2788 Squadron and Sergeant Cheetham of 4337 Flight were all mentioned in despatches.

In addition, the senior RAF Regiment officer, Lieutenant-Colonel H. M. Salmon, was promoted to the rank of Colonel. All in all, a reasonably satisfactory recognition of the achievements of the RAF Regiment squadrons and flights in the six-month long campaign which expelled the Axis forces from the North African shores.

Colonel Salmon immediately began to concentrate his units for reorganization and retraining in preparation for the next phase of the war in the Mediterranean – the invasion of Sicily and the assault on Italy. All five field squadrons concentrated at La Marsa under the control of the "RAF Regiment (North Africa) Wing Headquarters" which Colonel Salmon had formed and established on his own initiative. It set the pattern for the two ad hoc wing HQs which were formed in Sicily later in the year, and preceded the thirty-eight 'official' wing HQs which Air Ministry was to establish in 1944 and 1945. As there were now thirty-four independent AA flights in North Africa, which would be an inefficient use of resources in the campaigns which lay ahead, the Air Ministry approved Colonel Salmon's proposal to reorganize the personnel and equipment of the AA flights into eleven LAA squadrons. These were duly formed in May and June 1943 and numbered from 2860 to 2870.

The plan for the invasion of Sicily included forces from the United Kingdom (among which there were a number of RAF Regiment squadrons) as well as those from the victorious 1st and 8th Armies in North Africa. The air forces which were assembled for this operation were now designated as the North African Tactical Air Force, to which were assigned six of the sixteen Regiment squadrons in Eastern Air Command. These were 2721, 2771 and 2825 Field Squadrons and 2860, 2861 and 2862 LAA Squadrons.

The surrender of the Italian garrison on the island of Lampedusa, between Tunis and Malta, after heavy and sustained bombing over several weeks, resulted in 2774 Field and 2864 LAA Squadrons being deployed there to occupy the island under the command of the British military governor, an RAF wing commander. At the same time, it was considered that the airfield on the island of Gozo, although close to the heavily defended island of Malta, required its own low-level air defence during the build-up of the forces assembling there for the invasion of Sicily. Accordingly, 2862 LAA Squadron sailed from Sousse to Malta, and then made the short crossing to Gozo, being replaced in the invasion force for Sicily by 2864 Squadron, which was then withdrawn from Lampedusa, but not before it had acquired sufficient Italian 20mm Breda anti-aircraft guns to re-equip the squadron. Not only was their performance superior to the British Hispanos but they also had self-destructing high-explosive ammunition which did not endanger friendly forces on the ground.

2744 Field Squadron was thus stranded on Lampedusa until late September when a ship could be sent to bring it back to North Africa. While waiting for this happy event – Mussolini had used the island as a political prison, and it remained a dismal place – a USAAF Mitchell bomber appeared one night and fired distress signals before crashing at the western end of the island. Regiment patrols found the navigator alive on the land and he reported that the other four members of the crew had left the aircraft by parachute while it was over the sea. Fortunately, 2744 Squadron had earlier salvaged an abandoned Italian naval launch and made it seaworthy. The squadron commander ordered it to put to sea at once and the crew of two Regiment airmen and an Italian engineer were able to rescue three American airmen from the surrounding waters. The search for the missing pilot continued all day, ending with the discovery of his body several miles from the shore. His funeral, with full military honours, was arranged by the squadron which received the thanks of the USAAF for all that it had done for the aircrew. Squadron Leader Grace, LAC Bruce and AC1 Burton were subsquently mentioned in despatches for their actions.

HM King George VI visited his forces in North Africa in June and the Regiment provided his personal escort during his tour of RAF stations. Royal guards of honour were mounted by Regiment squadrons for the King's arrival in Tripolitania and for his departure from Grombalia in Tunisia. At the end of the Royal visit Colonel Salmon spoke to his AOC, Air Marshal Elmhirst, and said that he thought the guards of honour had been "pretty good". The AOC's immediate response was, "They weren't just pretty good, they were damned good!"

## THE NORTH AFRICAN CAMPAIGN IN RETROSPECT

Operation *Torch* broke new ground in many ways: it was the first major amphibious assault operation of the war, it was a joint US/British operation and it involved transporting the invasion force in several hundred merchant ships over long distances of open sea where the enemy could deploy submarines and aircraft to intercept the assault force before it reached its objectives. The operational problems which faced the commanders were so formidable that it can be appreciated why the logistic organization did not receive the attention it should have. Algiers was too small a port to handle the vast amount of supplies and equipment which were carried from the mounting bases in the UK but, worst of all, the loading of vessels was haphazard and so poorly documented that units ashore in North Africa did not know which ships were carrying their equipment, what was in which vessel and when and where it had been unloaded on the dockside. It was a painful, but invaluable, lesson for the planning staffs and although the logistic arrangements for the invasion of Sicily the following year still left something to be desired, most of the problems had been overcome by the time of the Normandy landings in 1944.

The size and composition of the Regiment element in the RAF

contingent was, to put it mildly, experimental and it was indeed fortunate that an officer as innovative and determined as Morrey Salmon should have been appointed to be the senior RAF Regiment officer in the invasion force. Having won two MCs in an infantry battalion in France in the First World War, he was an experienced soldier and a natural leader, with a questioning approach to authority. Although nominally a staff officer, he regarded himself as "Commander RAF Regiment" in the theatre and became deeply involved in the way in which his officers, men and units were employed. It was due to his foresight that the mass of Regiment officers and airmen scattered ineffectually throughout other RAF units were reorganized into anti-aircraft flights, and that these, and the original AA flights, were later regrouped into LAA squadrons. He argued for the establishment of wing headquarters to co-ordinate the operations of two or more squadrons and the first Regiment wing HQ was formed in North Africa at his direction, without waiting for authority from the Air Ministry. He developed a close liaison with the Army and initiated the detachment of field squadrons to infantry battalions in the front line to raise both their combat skills and their morale.

In the short space of six months the RAF Regiment had proved its effectiveness in the support of air operations against a determined enemy and, having learned the lessons of the North African campaign, were ready to occupy and defend airfields and installations elsewhere in the Mediterranean as the campaign moved forward to Sicily, Italy, and beyond.

## SQUADRONS AND FLIGHTS IN NORTH AFRICA 1942-43

**2721 Field**, Formed Mildenhall February 1942 from 721 RAF Defence Squadron. Algiers November 1942 – Cap Serrat – Medjez-el-Bab. Awards: 4 MID. To Italy Dec 1943.

**2774 Field**, Formed Belton Park May 1942 from 744 RAF Defence Squadron. Algiers November 1942 – Medjez el Bab – Bizerta – Lampedusa. Awards: 6 MID. To Italy Dec 1943.

**2771 Field** – Formed Cleave April 1942 from 771 RAF Defence Squadron. Algiers November 1942 – Bizerta. Awards: 2 MID. To Italy Dec 1943.

**2788 Field** – Formed Belton Park March 1942 from 788 RAF Defence Squadron. Algiers November 1942-Cap Serrat-Cap Bon-Tunis. Awards: 1 MC +1 MID. To Italy Dec 1943.

**2825 Field** – Formed Booker February 1942 from 825 RAF Defence Squadron. Algiers November 1942 – Maison Blanche – Constantine – Souk el Khemis – Kairouan. Awards: 1 MID. To Italy Dec 1943.

**4088 Independent AA Flight:** Formed Douglas IoM August 1942-Algiers November 42- La Marsa May 43.

**4089 Independent AA Flight:** Formed Douglas IoM August 1942-Algiers November 1942-Bone-La Marsa May 1943.

**4090 Independent AA Flight:** Formed Douglas IoM August 1942-Algiers November 1942. La Marsa May 1943. Awards: 3 MID.

**4091 Independent AA Flight:** Formed Douglas IoM August 1942-Algiers November 1942 – Medjez el Bab – Ferryville-La Marsa May 1943.

**4092 Independent AA Flight:** Formed Douglas IoM August 1942-Algiers November 1942-Cap Serrat – Medjez el Bab – Gharmart May 1943.

Nos.4337-4360 Independent AA Flights were formed in North Africa in February 1943 from RAF Regiment personnel within the theatre. Awards: 1 MC, 1 MM, 1 MID.

All AA Flights (4088-4092 & 4337-4360) were reorganized into the following 11 LAA squadrons in May/June 1943:

**2860 LAA** – Formed La Marsa from 4088, 4338 & 4337 AA Flts. To Italy September 1943

**2861 LAA** – Formed La Marsa from 4090, 4091 & 4337 AA Flts. To Italy February 1944

**2862 LAA** – Formed La Marsa from 4092, 4344 & 4339 AA Flts. To Malta June 1943

**2863 LAA** – Formed Gharmart from 4092, 4346 & 4339 AA Flts. To Italy December 1943

**2864 LAA** – Formed Grombalia from 4341, 4347 & 4356 AA Flts. To Italy June 1943

**2865 LAA** – Formed Bone from 4089, 4342 & 4351 AA Flts. To Italy October 1943

**2866 LAA** – Formed Setif from 4345, 4350 & 4352 AA Flts. To Italy December 1943

**2867 LAA** – Formed Phillipeville from 4343, 4349 & 4345 AA Flts. To Italy October 1943

**2868 LAA** – Formed Protville from 4348, 4349 & 4353 AA Flts. To Italy September 1943

**2869 LAA** – Formed La Sebala from 4355, 4357 & 4358 AA Flts. To Italy November 1943

**2870 LAA** – Formed Maison Blanche from 4354, 4358 & 4360 AA Flts. Disbanded January 1944

CHAPTER FIVE

# THE MIDDLE EAST 1942-46

The pattern of warfare which developed in the open spaces of the Western Desert was one in which armies able to exploit the advantages of speed, mobility and firepower had a decisive advantage over opponents who did not possess these attributes. In the opening stages of the desert campaigns, the British had outmanoeuvred and outgunned the Italians, but when the Germans arrived in North Africa to reinforce their allies, the British found themselves at a marked disadvantage. The armour, anti-tank artillery and tactical mobility of the Afrika Korps presented a challenge which the British commanders could only deal with by resorting to prepared defensive positions held by the less mobile infantry formations which predominated in the 8th Army at that stage.

Air power was one means of breaking this impasse and it was therefore the key to British success in the desert war. Demands for tactical air support had to be met without delay if they were to be effective and it was therefore necessary to base fighter aircraft as far forward as possible to achieve this. These forward landing grounds were often remote from, and usually undefended by, the Army divisions which were deployed to counter the enemy's dispositions on the ground. In 1940, however, the RAF had still not appreciated the interdependence of air operations and secure bases and had few reservations about placing its two armoured car companies in the Middle East under Army command to reinforce the armoured car regiments carrying out reconnaissance ahead of the 8th Army's main positions.

In the disastrous battles of 1941-42 in the Western Desert, the RAF lost aircraft to ground and air attacks on its forward landing grounds and the subsequent investigation into the campaign concluded that "we must have security on the ground if we are to operate effectively in the air" – but did not provide any answers towards the solution of that problem. The success of the Long Range Desert Group's raids against German and Italian airfields, in which over 400 Axis aircraft were destroyed, were uncomfortable reminders to the air staff that the Desert Air Force was equally vulnerable to similar attacks by the enemy's special forces, such as the Burckhardt Group, in addition to the more conventional forms of attack by aircraft and by groups of armour and mobile infantry looking for soft targets.

The Middle East Command had maintained the agreed inter-service policy which stipulated that the Army was responsible for providing the ground and air defence for RAF airfields and installations in the combat zone. As in other operational theatres, however, this commitment was to be constrained by the Army's shortage of manpower and its primary commitment to the land battle, both of which had often combined to leave the forward landing grounds unprotected and open to attack.

The RAF's ground defence resources in the Middle East in 1942 consisted of two armoured car companies, the locally-enlisted Levy forces in Iraq and Aden, and a number of RAF ground gunners, equipped only with small arms, who were distributed among RAF stations, wings and squadrons on a random basis to provide anti-aircraft defence, usually with World War I vintage Lewis guns. As these obsolescent weapons were found to be ineffective in the ground-to-air role, the Ground Gunners attached to flying units on forward airfields were often diverted to ground defence tasks, for which they were neither equipped nor trained. From the RAF's viewpoint the local defence situation had become critical, but the best which could be done was to obtain the Army's confirmation of the agreement to allocate 4,500 troops for the defence of airfields in the forward areas. This reinforcement was always subject to the condition that they could always be withdrawn without notice in the event of a major attack by the enemy, which was, of course, the time when they would be needed most by the Air Force.

Nos 1 and 2 Armoured Car Companies, which had been formed in Iraq in 1922, were still using World War I pattern Rolls-Royce armoured cars and the total strength of both companies was little more that one hundred officers and airmen. They did not form part of the RAF Regiment and retained their separate identities throughout the war. In the early phases of the desert campaign these units had been detached to the Army but once the threat to forward airfields was recognized, they reverted to RAF command and were used to supplement the RAF's very limited ground defence capability. Although the two armoured car companies performed prodigious tasks with inadequate equipment, their small numbers and outdated vehicles made it impossible for them to provide anything approaching adequate protection for the increasing number of forward airfields in the Western Desert.

At the beginning of 1942 there were some 3,800 Ground Gunners within the Middle East; a year later the total had risen to 8,100, of whom 3,200 were serving in Aden, Cyprus, Iraq, Malta, East Africa, the Levant and the Sudan. Scattered among RAF units, this amorphous body of airmen lacked a command structure, organization, leadership and adequate training and equipment for its war role. Despite their limited operational effectiveness, the presence of Ground Gunners on stations came to be regarded by senior RAF officers as an important reservoir of manpower for the various unestablished tasks which were deemed to be vitally important to the administrative well-being of the Air Force and Ground Gunners were, more often than not, misemployed on mundane administrative tasks.

In September 1941 a small ground defence staff of three RAF officers had been established at HQ Middle East Air Force with the remit to plan passive defence measures, such as camouflage, dispersal and protection against high explosive and chemical attack, for RAF installations in the Middle East. A passive defence training school was formed at Helwan, in the Canal Zone, but no provision was made for active defence training. This structure changed soon after the formation of the Regiment in February 1942, when RAF Regiment officers arrived in the theatre and staff officers were established at command and group headquarters. As officer and NCO instructors became available, ground defence training schools were established in the Western Desert, the Canal Zone and at Amman in Jordan. Despite the continuing pressure of operational commitments, the former Ground Gunners, who were now Regiment airmen, in the Desert Air Force's flying wings and squadrons were retrained in situ while those in the peripheral areas were drawn into the training cycle and replaced by locally-enlisted levies. The role of Regiment units was defined as the occupation and protection of forward airfields, together with the provision and manning of anti-aircraft weapons of up to 20mm calibre, and the training system was designed to meet these criteria.

The first target was to reorganize the 8,100 Regiment airmen in the theatre into 225 anti-aircraft flights, each of one junior officer and thirty-six airmen, but before this could be completed the Air Ministry in London countered the HQ Middle East claim for an increase in Regiment strength to 9,000 by imposing a manpower ceiling of 4,800 Regiment officers and airmen on the Command. While the respective staffs battled to achieve what each believed to be a more realistic figure, the immediate problem was the shortage of Regiment officers, which was reflected in twenty staff and 115 flight commander posts being unfilled, with a considerable effect on operational capability at unit level. As no officers could be spared from the UK, the training school at Amman was expanded into an OCTU and NCOs and airmen already in the Middle East were selected for officer training and subsequent commissioning.

While the formation of RAF Regiment flights and squadrons was in progress, the Afrika Korps began its advance on Cairo and the Desert

Air Force had to concentrate all its efforts on supporting the 8th Army to halt the German attack before Rommel could reach the Suez Canal. A further complication at this time was the pressing need to break the Axis blockade of Malta and deliver much-needed supplies and reinforcements to the beleagured island. Two convoys were assembled in June 1942 – a western one at Gibraltar and an eastern one at Alexandria, totalling seventeen merchant ships with no fewer than sixty-six escort vessels. Such was the intensity of German and Italian air, surface and submarine attack that only two merchant ships, which were both from the western convoy, finally reached Malta with their cargoes.

The eastern convoy, which sailed from Alexandria, carried an improvised RAF Regiment force, drawn from the Middle East Command manpower pool and designated Clara Squadron, to man the anti-aircraft guns on the merchant ships. In fact, none of the vessels in this convoy reached Malta and those ships which were not sunk were forced to turn back by shortage of fuel after enduring continuous attacks by enemy aircraft, surface vessels and submarines for over four days. AC1 Richard O'Neill of Clara Squadron was seriously wounded while firing an anti-aircraft gun against attacking aircraft but this did not prevent him from rescuing two of his colleagues who were in the water with him after their ship went down. His actions were recognized by the unusual award of a Royal Navy decoration – the Distinguished Service Medal – to a member of the RAF Regiment, shortly before be was invalided in the following year as a result of his wounds.

In September 1942 the situation in the Western Desert had stabilized and the formation of operational Regiment units continued with a centralized training school which was moved from Ma'aten Bagush in Egypt to Shallufa in the Canal Zone. 231 independent anti-aircraft flights were now needed to provide the required level of defence, but time, manpower and equipment shortages made it impossible to form – and train – this number of units by the hoped-for date. Because of these problems, only fifty-seven of the new AA flights were ready in time to accompany the flying squadrons and wings as they moved westwards after the battle of Alamein in October 1942, but by the end of 1942 the training machine had produced an adequate number of RAF Regiment AA flights to meet the needs of the flying squadrons and wings in the Western Desert.

As the 8th Army advanced towards Tunis, the fighter wings of the Desert Air Force and their attached RAF Regiment AA flights moved forward, sometimes with one or other of the armoured car companies. The leading Regiment units reached the landing grounds at Daba and Fuka, between Alamein and Mersa Matruh, and seized them from the

*RAF Regiment flight in the Western Desert – 1943.* (Crown Copyright/MOD)

enemy, taking several hundred prisoners in the process. In November a column of RAF vehicles was halted at the foot of the Halfaya Pass, on the Libyan frontier with Egypt, when it was attacked by a group of Ju88 bombers which approached at low level from the coast nearby. LAC George Bullen of 166 AA Flight RAF Regiment, attached to 239 Fighter Wing, engaged the leading aircraft and the first burst from his 20mm Hispano gun destroyed the bomber's starboard engine and sent the enemy aircraft out of control into the sea.

In December 166 AA Flight was defending the forward airfield at El Agheila, between Benghazi and Tripoli, when a Ju88 appeared through a break in the clouds and prepared to attack the numerous RAF aircraft dispersed on the airfield. Bullen again manned his 20mm gun and promptly shot down the German aircraft, which crashed with the loss of all its crew. Although awards were subsequently made for earlier acts of gallantry by other Regiment personnel, the Military Medal awarded to LAC Bullen for these two actions was the first such award to be announced for a member of the RAF Regiment and he received a personal message of congratulations from the Under Secretary of State for Air.

In January 1943 the race for Tripoli began and the Regiment flights in 243 Fighter Wing were concentrated and ordered to secure three vital installations in the town for the RAF. These were the Uaddan Hotel (for use as the RAF Officers' Club), the Fiat garage (as the RAF MT servicing facility) and, of course, Castel Benito airfield for the exclusive use of the RAF and the USAAF. It was a close-run thing but Flight Lieutenants Richard Cox and Stan Rhodes, and their AA flights, had seized all three objectives for the Air Force before the Army entered the town.

As with many other innovations in later campaigns, the Ground/Air Landmarks (GALs) which were used extensively in Italy had their precursors in the Desert Air Force's experience in the Western Desert. The initial use of heavy bombers to provide support for the Army had been marred by incidents in which the bombs fell on friendly troops instead of the enemy and an improvised GAL system was introduced to mark the positions of forward troops for friendly aircraft. Four-gallon petrol tins, with one side cut out and hurricane lamps placed inside, were set out at ten-yard intervals along the notional bomb line, and this contributed something towards improving the effectiveness of this form of air support, albeit at rather less cost than the de luxe version which was later developed for use in Italy.

From the outset the setting out of GALs was a Regiment responsibility and the teams carrying out these tasks were given special priority on the roads leading to the front line. This led, on one occasion at least, to a brief encounter between a junior Regiment officer and the GOC-in-C Middle East when a GAL vehicle convoy, its three-ton trucks filled with hundreds of empty petrol tins, hurricane lamps and paraffin containers, was overtaken and stopped by a military police jeep. Flying Officer Duncan Lavers leaned out of the cab of his 15cwt truck to remonstrate with the MPs for stopping a priority convoy when he heard a stentorian voice boom out, "Get your vehicles off the road, sir," and turned his head to see a bristling General Sir Harold Alexander in the staff car behind the jeep. On that occasion, at least, the GAL team involved recognized that someone else had higher priority than they did!

Flying Officer Lavers was reputed to have used the incident later as a conversation-stopper beginning, "As I said to General Alexander the other day...".

As the campaign in the Western Desert continued it became clear that the fragmentation of anti-aircraft defences into small flights was both inefficient and uneconomical and the imposed reductions on Regiment manpower in the Command made it essential to reorganize these resources into squadrons if the best use was to be made of a smaller number of RAF Regiment officers and airmen. Twenty-four AA flights were assembled at Castel Benito, near Tripoli, in February 1943 to form the first four of these squadrons which were numbered from 2930 to 2933. Each squadron had an establishment of eight officers and 219 airmen with a headquarters, three rifle flights and three anti-aircraft flights each of eight 20mm Hispano guns.

The practical experience gained by the RAF Regiment in the Torch campaign in North Africa, which ended with the Axis surrender in Tunis in May 1943, had shown that the mixed rifle/LAA squadron organization would be too cumbersome and inflexible for future operations. HQ Middle East therefore reissued their unit establishments and formed a total of 36 separate field and LAA squadrons from the remaining independent AA flights, which were disbanded to provide the necessary manpower. The LAA squadrons were organized into four flights, each with six 20mm Hispano guns while the field squadrons contained three rifle flights, a support flight with four 3″ mortars and a flight of six armoured cars for reconnaissance and escort tasks.

However, despite the large geographical area which the Middle East Command covered, its Regiment squadrons were destined to play only a supporting role from May 1943 until the end of the war, when Regiment squadrons began to return to the Middle East from Italy and Austria in increasing numbers as a result of the worsening internal security situation in the mandated territory of Palestine from 1945 onwards. There were to be some small-scale diversions in 1943/44, such as an improvised expedition in the Aegean and sabre-rattling in the hope of encouraging Turkey to join the Allied side against the Axis, but with the ejection of the Afrika Korps from the North African littoral the threat to British forces and installations in most of the Command was greatly reduced and the theatre which had borne the brunt of British military operations from 1940 to 1943 was overshadowed by the emphasis on what were now the more important campaigns in Europe and the Far East.

By the end of 1943 the RAF Regiment staff structure in the Middle East Air Force had expanded and was considerably larger than that in the North African Air Force, which was destined to become the Mediterranean Air Force and the major player in the theatre. The Command Defence Officer in the Middle East was Colonel J. B. Rosher DSO* MC, a London lawyer who had distinguished himself in command of a Durham Light Infantry battalion in France in the First

*Sqn Ldr Cox and officers of 'B' Squadron at Castel Benito in 1943.* (R Cox)

World War. Although the Regiment staff officers followed conventional RAF procedure and refrained from direct involvement with the Regiment squadrons in the command, Colonel Rosher did not hesitate to deal with the unusual situation which arose in Sicily when three of his squadrons were deployed there without a controlling headquarters. He immediately detached his deputy, Lieutenant-Colonel C D Bowdery, also of the DLI, to Sicily to establish the wing headquarters which was formed to exercise control over those units and co-ordinate their operations until a more permanent organization could be established.

## THE BATTLE FOR COS

One of the strategic options for the Allied campaign in the Mediterranean theatre was to take Sicily and then by-pass Italy by seizing the Dodecanese Islands in the Aegean and outflanking the German positions in Greece and the Cyclades while threatening the southern approaches to the Balkans. This was Operation *Accolade* – a bold move, which might have brought Turkey into the war on the allied side and drawn German forces away from both the eastern and western fronts – and avoided the slow and costly task of fighting step by step for 500 miles northwards along the narrow Italian peninsula, which provided an ideal defensive front for the German army. However, the plan for *Accolade* was based on an overwhelming concentration of force, and the achievement of air superiority, which called for 235 naval and merchant ships, twenty-one infantry battalions and armoured regiments, thirty-three bomber squadrons, forty-one squadrons of tactical aircraft, 150 transport aircraft – and six RAF Regiment squadrons – in an assault on Rhodes, Scarpanto and Cos as a prelude to a drive northwards past the Dardenelles towards the Balkans and Greece. To that extent, it was clearly incompatible with an invasion of Italy.

The Sicilian campaign ended in August 1943 and the invasion of Italy began in September, absorbing most of the forces which had been earmarked for Accolade. Following the Italian armistice, and the accession of Italy to the Allied side, the War Cabinet put pressure on the C-in-C Middle East to broaden the war in the eastern Mediterranean by attacking the German forces in the Aegean which had been deprived of Italian support. The justification for this was the belief that the enemy forces in that area would have lost their offensive capability and would not present serious opposition to the much smaller British forces which were left to carry out a reduced version of the original plan.

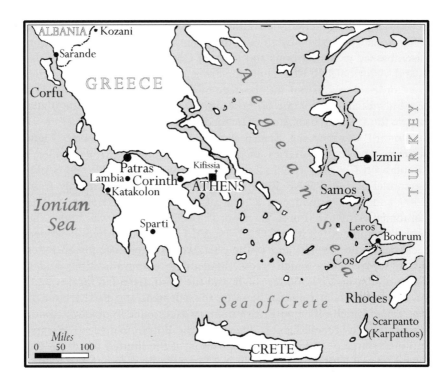

As the forces available to the Middle East Command were insufficient to achieve the original objectives of *Accolade* – the capture of the German-held islands of Rhodes and Scarpanto – it was decided to seize the islands of Samos, Leros and Cos instead, using Cos, which was the only one of the three with an airstrip – as the main base for a later assault on Rhodes and further expansion northwards in the Aegean. Although the Italian garrison on Cos could be relied upon to welcome British forces, the island had an undeveloped airfield and an inadequate harbour. It was therefore a poor substitute for Rhodes, with its good airfields and excellent port facilities.

On 13 September 1943, Major Lord Jellicoe, with Long Range Desert Group, Special Air Service and Special Boat Service detachments, took possession of Cos and on 15 and 16 September two flights of 2909 LAA Squadron were flown in from Ramat David in Palestine and deployed their 20mm Hispanos on the rocky outcrops around the airstrip at Antimachia towards the western end of the island. German air strikes began on the 18th and over the next three days 2909 Squadron destroyed and damaged eight enemy aircraft for the loss of two airman killed and three seriously wounded. There was a lull of several days in the enemy air attacks, during which the remainder of 2909 Squadron arrived by air, and the majority of 2901 Field Squadron disembarked at the harbour and town of Cos, on the eastern tip of the island. A further five Regiment squadrons, from Palestine and Cyprus, were ordered to Cos but the shortage of shipping was such than only a few individuals from some of those units were able to reach the island before the German attack overwhelmed the defences.

On 3rd October the British Army (1st Battalion Durham Light Infantry and two batteries of 1st LAA Regiment Royal Artillery) strength on Cos was 1,095 all ranks. There were 235 RAF and SAAF personnel and 229 RAF Regiment officers and airmen, mainly from 2909 and 2901 Squadrons, a total of 464 officers and airmen. The combined Army/Air Force garrison of 1,559 all ranks was under the overall command of the CO of 1st DLI. He established defended localities at the airfield and at the port, which were over fifteen miles apart, separated by rough tracks, inadequate communications and a range of hills up to 2,500 feet high, and the third defended locality with his headquarters at Lambia, between the salt pans and the harbour. It was a plan which reflected British military experience in quelling minor insurgencies by rebellious factions within the Empire between the wars, but it was a tactically unsound disposition of the limited forces on the island to deal with an aggressively-led, numerically superior and battle-experienced German force of all arms, operating with overwhelming air support from fighter, bomber and transport aircraft.

An emergency landing strip had been constructed near Lambia on the northern coast and the RAF Regiment was spread among Antimachia airfield (one flight 2909 with eleven 20mm guns), Lambia (one flight 2909 with eight 20mm guns) and the town and harbour of Cos (one flight 2909 with five 20mm guns and two field flights from 2901). The Royal Artillery had one battery of eighteen 40mm Bofors guns at the airfield, while the other battery was split, with nine of its 40mm guns at the airstrip and the remaining seven 40mm guns defending the harbour and town. Of the three infantry companies of 1st DLI, one was deployed at Antimachia on the west and another at Cos harbour on the east, while the third company and battalion HQ was located to the north near Lambia. Air defence was provided by Spitfires of No.74 Squadron Royal Air Force and No.7 Squadron South African Air Force, dispersed on the airfield and at the emergency landing ground.

While there was never any possibility of defending the long coastline against a seaborne landing, the fragmentation of the defenders among three widely separated defended localities, too far apart for any one to be able to give mutual support to another, reduced the effectiveness of the defence to one-third of its total strength and gave an enemy the opportunity to pick off the isolated defensive positions by concentrating superior forces on each in turn. The clear lessons of the attack on Crete, with the loss of the airfield at Maleme as the turning-point in the battle, had obviously been forgotten: had all the British forces been concentrated to defend the airfield at Antimachia, the German attack could have been withstood for much longer, almost certainly for long enough to enable the RAF to re-establish local air superiority to cover the reinforcement of the island and eliminate the enemy's initial tactical advantage. As it was, the Germans were able to use the captured airfield for their own purposes within 12 hours of coming ashore.

Tactical surprise was achieved by the German ships which landed a battle group of between two and three thousand troops at three points on the coast of Cos at dawn on 3 October. German air superiority had prevented continuing British surveillance and effective naval or air attacks on the convoy which brought the invasion force from Crete and the defenders had a further unwelcome surprise when parachute troops from bases in Greece were dropped near the airfield at Antimachia and the airstrip at Lambia to support the seaborne force in seizing these key objectives. It was almost a carbon copy of the successful German attack on Crete, which had brought the importance of airfield defence and air superiority to the attention of the British government, two years earlier.

Continuous air cover from fighters and bombers supported the German infantry and artillery in attacks on the airfield and the satellite airstrip and by mid-afternoon most of the LAA guns had either been destroyed or were out of ammunition. The surviving British personnel fell back on the town of Cos and the fighting continued throughout the night, but by the following morning the Germans were in control of the whole island. Some of the British garrison had escaped in small boats from the harbour to Turkey, a few miles away, while others had taken to the hills, from where they continued the battle until they were captured or managed to escape from the island. Corporal Neale, who was in one of the 2901 Squadron flights positioned to defend the harbour at Cos, was able to escape under cover of darkness, with two other airmen and several soldiers, in a small, leaky boat. After continuous bailing to stay afloat, and hard rowing with improvised oars, they reached the Turkish coast near Bodrum the following morning. From there they were later evacuated to Cyprus, where Neale and his two colleagues joined 2924 Field Squadron at Paphos.

In the following weeks a number of the soldiers and airmen who had evaded capture and were hiding in the hills were contacted by SBS patrols and those who escaped from the island in this way included seventeen Regiment personnel. However, Squadron Leader Kilgallin, OC 2909 Squadron, and the remaining Regiment officers and airmen, of whom only five were unwounded, were taken prisoner and spent the rest of the war in POW camps in Germany. One of the 2909 Squadron airmen taken prisoner was LAC Charles Eyles who was sent to Stalag IVB near Leipzig with his colleagues. In April 1945, Eyles and three other airmen who were working at a local factory evaded their guards and started to make their way westwards towards the advancing US armies. When they finally reached an American armoured column, the first officer to whom they spoke was General Patton himself, whom they readily identified from the two pearl-handled revolvers in his waistbelt.

Army and RAF officers who escaped from Cos paid fulsome tributes to the gallantry and determination of the Regiment force which had fought so well against overwhelming odds in the brief campaign. On his return to duty after the war, Kilgallin made strong representations for due recognition of the actions of his men during the battle. Continuing to press the case long after he had been demobilized and returned to civilian life, his persistence was rewarded by the award of the Military Medal to Warrant Officer Payne and LAC Tucker, and mentions in despatches for two officers and five airmen, all of 2909 Squadron, in 1948.

The official report on the Aegean operation highlighted a number of failings which had affected the RAF Regiment on Cos. Firstly, command and control of the RAF defences was hampered by the failure to establish a Regiment wing HQ on the island at the outset. There were no standard scales of equipment for the squadrons tasked for the operation and 2909 and 2901 Squadrons had been sent to Cos without maps or vehicles. The 20mm Hispanos had been issued to 2909 immediately before emplaning for Cos without pre-firing checks being carried out and some guns were found to be unserviceable on arrival. The rocky terrain prevented guns from being dug in and the lack of protection for the gun detachments resulted in casualties, for whom there were no replacements. All in all it was greatly to the credit of all concerned that the Regiment was able to fight so effectively for as long as it did.

As far as Middle East Command was concerned, the abortive campaign once again demonstrated the difficulties involved in attacking an enemy able to operate on interior lines, with the ability to concentrate his forces easily and achieve surprise by swift and decisive action. Apart from reminding those concerned of the ever-present influence of the principles of war, the operation proved yet again that an enemy which achieved even temporary air superiority over the area of operations would inevitably defeat the opposing British naval and military forces.

## REORGANIZATION WITHIN THE COMMAND

After the Cos débâcle HQ Middle East Command ordered all the remaining Regiment personnel in the theatre to concentrate at Aleppo for reorganization and retraining. The result was a force of 8 field squadrons and 20 LAA squadrons, the latter equipped with a mix of 20mm Hispano and 40mm Bofors guns. The remaining officers and airmen were formed into a training squadron and two second-line squadrons, bringing the total force level to thirty-one squadrons of one sort or another. This did not last for long and the pressure for more manpower in the United Kingdom prior to the invasion of France led to the disbandment of ten of these squadrons and the return of their personnel to the UK. The subsequent reduction of the Command's RAF Regiment establishment to a maximum of 5,300 all ranks made a further period of reorganization and retraining essential to make the best possible use of these limited resources.

In May 1944 Middle East Command was ordered to mount Operation *Turpitude* – a major show of force in northern Syria with two aims: to mislead the Germans into thinking that an invasion of northern Greece was imminent, and secondly to encourage the Turkish government to believe that substantial Allied forces were available to support Turkey should that country decide to declare war on Germany. Three field squadrons and one LAA squadron, together with an RAF armoured car company, were deployed to the Turkish border to

*Colonel JB Rosher DSO MC inspecting 1322 Wing in Egypt prior to redeployment to Italy in 1944.* (N Salmon)

demonstrate British capabilities. A further three LAA squadrons were put on standby for Operation *Saturn* in case it became necessary to reinforce airfields in Turkey. As it happened, both the operations lapsed as the successful landings in Normandy in June 1944 moved the focus of the military and political situation from the Middle East to Europe.

By 1944 there was no longer a war role in Middle East Command for Regiment units and in that year nine squadrons were redeployed to Italy to join the seven which had been sent to Sicily and Italy in 1943. Those squadrons remaining in the Middle East had all been disbanded by mid-1944 and there were no Regiment units in the theatre from then until 1319 Wing from Italy and 1321 Wing from Austria were redeployed to Palestine in December 1945 and March 1946 respectively. Among the first squadrons to arrive in this way were three which had been formed in the Middle East during the war. Their roles included internal security duties and the protection of RAF installations against increasing levels of violence. From then onwards, the steadily growing RAF Regiment presence in the eastern Mediterranean was to be committed to a variety of operational tasks in Palestine, Transjordan, Iraq, the Canal Zone and Cyprus.

## THE MIDDLE EAST CAMPAIGN IN RETROSPECT

In many ways the formation, training and equipping of RAF Regiment flights and squadrons was more difficult in the Middle East than elsewhere. In 1942 the Command was fully engaged in a battle for survival as the German and Italian forces, ably led by Rommel, threatened the existence of the Army and Air Force in Egypt and it was not until the pattern of advances and retreats had been broken by the stubborn defensive battle of first Alamein that adequate resources could be made available for the restructuring of RAF Regiment resources.

Thus Regiment anti-aircraft flights had to be committed piecemeal to the fighter, fighter/bomber and light bomber wings which moved forward with the Army after the battle of Alamein and it was only as that campaign approached its end that field and LAA squadrons could be formed from the available manpower in the theatre. But, once the Axis forces had surrendered in May 1943, there was no real role for the Regiment units in the Middle East. There were diversions, of course, such as the abortive attempt to seize islands in the Dodecanese which resulted in the disaster on Cos and demonstrations in Syria to encourage Turkey to enter the war on the Allied side. But from 1943 onwards the role of Middle East Command was to provide Regiment field and LAA squadrons as reinforcements for the Central Mediterranean theatre.

As the principal pre-war overseas headquarters, the Command had a well-established staff structure in the Canal Zone and the establishment of RAF Regiment staff officers followed the pattern which already existed in the headquarters. With the emphasis on training all RAF personnel in active and passive defence measures as well as setting up the infrastructure for the training of RAF Regiment gunners, NCOs and officers, a large staff organization, headed by a group captain post but filled by a colonel, was formed. In addition, RAF Regiment officers were established on all operational units, particularly the flying wings, to advise on defence in the field.

From 1944 until the end of the war, the RAF Regiment staff organization in the Middle East was undoubtedly as efficient and comprehensive as the remainder of the impressive headquarters establishment, but it added little to the operational effectiveness of the Regiment units which had been formed in the Command but were now deployed in operational theatres elsewhere. In March 1945 the flow of Regiment squadrons back to the Middle East began as the internal security situation in the mandated territory of Palestine started to deteriorate and where only No.2 Armoured Car Company was available initially to defend RAF airfields and installations. When, in 1948, the British government finally abandoned the attempt to maintain law and order in that part of the Middle East, the Regiment returned to the Canal Zone from Palestine, but that is another story.

## WING HQs IN THE MIDDLE EAST 1943-1946

**500** Formed Hadera for Operation *Accolade* September 1943.
Disbanded October 1943.
**1322** Formed Aboukir August 1944. To Italy August 1944.
**1319** From Italy to Palestine December 1945.
**1320** From Austria to Palestine March 1946.
**1321** From Greece to Palestine March 1945.

## SQUADRONS IN THE MIDDLE EAST 1943-46

**2900 LAA** – Formed Heliopolis May 1943. Gaza-Hadera-
Alexandria. To Italy May 44.
**2901 Field** – Formed Abu Sueir May 1943. Beirut- 500 Wing –
(*Accolade*) – Cos – Castelrosso – Cyprus – Famagusta
– Lakatamia – Haifa – Hadera – Aleppo. March 1944
Disbanded.
**2902 Field** – Formed Helwan May 1943. Beirut – 500 Wing
(*Accolade)* – Aleppo – Kabrit – Gaza – (*Turpitude*) –
Hadera.
To Italy August 1944. To Palestine December 1945.
**2903 Field** – Formed Aboukir May 1943. Beirut – Hadera – 500
Wing *(Accolade)* – Aleppo. March 1944 Disbanded.
**2904 Field** – Formed Shallufa May 1943. To Sicily – (*Husky*) – July 1943.
**2905 Field** – Formed El Khanka May 43. Mersa Matruh – Tobruk –
Benghazi – Tripoli – Kairouan – Hani West – Hammamet
– Tunis. To Italy November 1943.
**2906 Field** – Formed Shallufa May 1943. To Sicily – (*Husky*) – July
1943.
**2907 LAA** – Formed Cairo West May 1943. Hadera – 500 Wing
(*Accolade)* – Haifa – Castelrosso – Haifa – Aleppo –
Hadera – (*Saturn*) – Almaza – Mersa Matruh – Aboukir.
To Italy June 1944.
**2908 Field** – Formed Khataba May 1943. Hadera – 500 Wing (*Accolade)*
– Aleppo – Kabrit – (*Turpitude*) – Aleppo – Alexandria.
To Italy August 1944. To Palestine March 1946. Lydda –
Ein Shemer.
**2909 LAA** – Formed Gianallis May 1943. Hadera – 500 Wing –
(*Accolade*) – Cos. Awards: 2 MM + 7 MID. Ceased to
exist 4 October 1943.
**2910 LAA** – Formed Idku May 1943. Hadera. May 1944 Disbanded.
**2911 Field** – Formed Mersa Matruh May 1943. March 1944
Disbanded.

**2912 LAA** – Formed Port Said May 1943. Gaza. April 1944 Disbanded.

**2913 LAA** – Formed El Agoud May 1943. Gaza – Hadera – Alexandria. To Italy July 1944.

**2914 LAA** – Formed Shallufa May 1943. Bersis – Tobruk – Apollonia. To Italy July 1944.

**2915 LAA** – Formed El Adem May 1943. Almaza – Hadera – Hose Ravi – Tura – Gaza. April 1944 Disbanded.

**2916 LAA** – Formed Gambut May 1943. Hadera – Gaza. To Italy May 1944.

**2917 LAA** – Formed Savoia May 1943. Alba – Apollonia. March 1944 Disbanded.

**2918 Field** – Formed Benina May 1943. Shallufa – Hadera – Aleppo – Minnick. LAA.Hadera (*Saturn*). April 1944 Disbanded.

**2919 Field** – Formed Berka May 1943. March 1944 Disbanded.

**2920 LAA** – Formed Gardabia May 1943. Misurata – Tripoli – Hadera – Damascus – Masmiya. May 1944 Disbanded.

**2921 LAA** – Formed Mellaha May 1943. Gaza East – Hadera. April 1944 Disbanded.

**2922 LAA** – Formed Misurata May 1943. Tripoli – Gaza East – Hadera. April 1944 Disbanded.

**2923 LAA** – Formed Castel Benito May 1943. Benina – Apollonia – Almaza. To Italy July 1944. To Palestine March 1945. Field. Ramleh – Jerusalem – Lydda – Ras el Ein. April 1946 Disbanded.

**2924 Field** – Formed Latakamia (Cyprus) May 1943 (with 22 light tanks). (*Accolade*) – Castelrosso – Aleppo – (*Turpitude*) – Kabrit. To Italy August 1944. To Palestine March 1945. Ramleh – Ras el Ein – Lydda.

**2925 LAA** – Formed Hadera May 1943. To Sicily July 1943 – *Husky*.

**2926 LAA** – Formed Benghazi May 1943. Hadera – Apollonia. To Italy June 1944.

**2927 LAA** – Formed Habbaniya (Iraq) May 1943. Benghazi – Apollonia. April 1944 Disbanded.

**2928 LAA** – Formed Habbaniya (Iraq) June 1943. Hadera. June 1944 Disbanded.

**2929 LAA** – Formed Habbaniya (Iraq) September 1943. Gaza East. January 1944 Disbanded.

**2930 LAA** – Formed Castel Benito February 1943 as "A" Squadron. Mareth – Gabes – Azizia – Benghazi – Khanka – Helwan – Gaza East – Hadera. April 1944 Disbanded.

**2931 LAA** – Formed Castel Benito March 1943 as "B" Squadron. Tripoli – Palestine. April 1944 Disbanded.

**2932 LAA** – Formed Castel Benito April 1943 as "C" Squadron. Gaza East – Beit Daras – (*Turpitude*) – Minnick. To Italy July 1944.

**2933 LAA** – Formed Castel Benito May 1943 as "D" Squadron. Berka – Lete (USAAF airfields) – Tura – Hadera – (*Saturn*) – Affise – Masmiya. To Italy July 1944.

**2934 LAA** – Formed Malta May 1943. Luqa – Hal Far – Ta'kali. To UK January 1944.

**2935 LAA** – Formed Aleppo May 1943. Hadera. June 1944 Disbanded.

**2969 Rifle** – From Italy April 1945. Palestine. Jerusalem – Petat Tiqva. April 1946 Disbanded.

**2717 Rifle** – From NW Europe October 1945 to Palestine. Ramleh – Petat Tiqva – Jerusalem.

**2721 Rifle** – From Italy December 1945 to Palestine. St Jean – Ein Shemer.

**2742 Rifle** – From NW Europe October 1945 to Palestine. Petat Tiqva – Ramat David.

**2771 Rifle** – From Austria March 1946 to Palestine. Ramat David – St Jean.

**2788 Rifle** – From Greece March 1945 to Palestine. Ramleh – Ein Shemer.

**2864 Rifle** – From Italy April 1945 to Palestine. Ramat David – Ramleh – Lydda.

# CHAPTER SIX

# THE CENTRAL MEDITERRANEAN
# 1942-45

## THE INVASION OF SICILY

The Allied invasion of Sicily, Operation *Husky*, began with an airborne assault on the night of 9/10 July 1943, and was followed by seaborne landings in the early hours of 10 July when the first Regiment squadrons – 2855 LAA from the UK and 2925 LAA from the Middle East went ashore. Unfortunately, the ship carrying most of 2855's guns, vehicles and unit equipment was sunk by enemy air attack and the squadron had a frustrating time until it had been re-equipped and was able to deploy at Pachino airfield alongside 2925 Squadron.

The second wave of Regiment squadrons landed on 19 July. These were four LAA squadrons from the UK: 2856,2857, 2858 and 2859, which were later joined by 2864 LAA from North Africa. Two field squadrons, 2904 and 2906, arrived from the Middle East and this force of nine independent squadrons was grouped into two RAF Regiment wings for command and control purposes. The two wings moved steadily forward as the enemy withdrew towards Messina and were the first British units to occupy the airfield at Catania. By the end of July the squadrons were deployed at Pachino, Lentini West, Scordia, Palagonia, Agnone, San Francesca and Lentini East. In August two more LAA squadrons, 2862 and 2868 from North Africa, landed at Palermo to defend the major airfield there.

The disparity among the squadrons from the United Kingdom, the Middle East and North Africa became obvious once they were all deployed together on an island in the same theatre. The non-interoperability of radio equipment and the limited scale of radios forced undue reliance on landline and telephone communications at squadron and wing level and the overall standard of individual and collective training varied considerably between squadrons from different commands. Unit equipment differed in type and quantity and administrative support was lacking in critical areas, for example; the UK squadrons had been committed to a malarial area without mosquito nets or prophylactic medication and 2857 Squadron's operational effectiveness was seriously reduced by numerous cases of malaria.

The two ad hoc wing headquarters which were formed for command and control purposes were "A" Wing, with 2855 & 2858 LAA and 2904

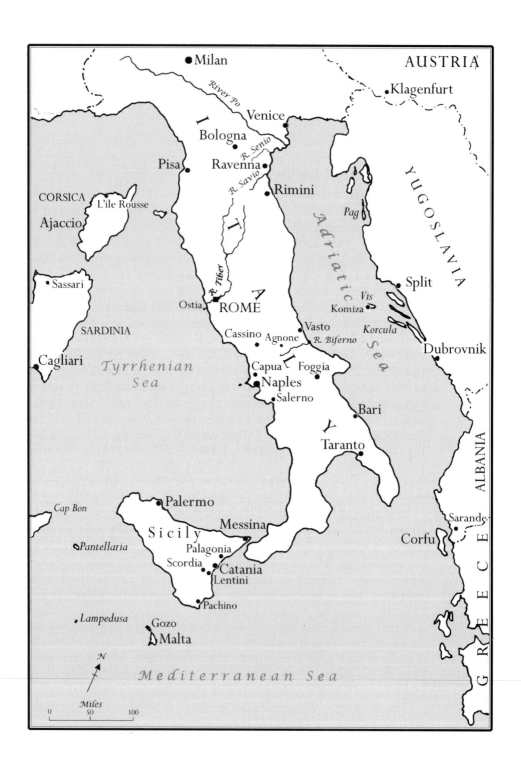

& 2906 Field Squadrons, and "B" Wing with 2856, 2857, 2859, 2925 and 2864 LAA Squadrons. "A" Wing was commanded by Lieutenant Colonel Bowdery from HQ Middle East and "B" Wing by Wing Commander Gould from the UK. At the same time air operations were being conducted by the RAF and USAAF through different, and separate air headquarters in North Africa and the Middle East. It was not until this unwieldy structure was rationalized and all the RAF Regiment squadrons in the Central Mediterranean theatre could be placed under the sole command of Colonel Salmon that operations could be directed in an efficient and militarily effective manner.

Although all the LAA squadrons in Sicily were equipped with the 20mm Hispano cannon, or, in one case at least, with captured Italian Breda 20mm guns, the crowded airspace and the proximity of airfields on the island soon revealed the weaknesses of the Hispanos in such conditions. It did not take long to discover that, as the 20mm ammunition was a mixture of ball and high explosive, neither of which destroyed itself in the air if it missed its target, 20mm rounds which fell on neighbouring airfields caused more casualties to personnel and damage to aircraft than did enemy air attacks. Colin Hope, a Regiment gunner in 2859 LAA Squadron, recalls that when his squadron engaged attacking German aircraft at Lentini East their 20mm HE shells fell on the adjoining airfield, destroying or damaging six Spitfires in the dispersal area there. The consequent restrictions placed on the LAA squadrons severely limited their usefulness in their primary AA role, but this added weight to the case made by Colonel Salmon for the re-equipment of his LAA squadrons with 40mm Bofors anti-aircraft guns and their self-destructing high explosive shells. It so happened that 2906 Field and 2925 LAA Squadrons followed 2859 LAA Squadron to Lentini East, where the restrictions on the use of their AA guns enabled enemy aircraft to attack their gun positions with ease, causing numerous casualties to the unfortunate gunners of those squadrons.

By the end of August the whole of Sicily was in Allied hands and the invasion of Italy was imminent. This weakened the position of the Italian government, which now became anxious to conclude an armistice with the British and American governments. To this end a three-engined Savoia Marchetti transport aircraft of the Regia Aeronautica, with Italian emissaries on board, landed at Palermo airfield to discuss these arrangements with the Allied Commander-in-Chief, Field Marshal Alexander. In order to preserve secrecy the only British unit, 2864 LAA Squadron, on the USAAF – operated airfield was ordered to secure the aircraft and its crew while its passengers were taken to the Field Marshal's headquarters.

The situation was thrown into disarray by the unexpected arrival of an American aircraft carrying Italian delegates from a similar meeting in Lisbon. They had been flown to Palermo from Algiers, on General Eisenhower's instructions, to join the Italian aircraft which the Americans believed had been sent to Palermo to take their Italian party back to Italy. The British Colonel escorting the Lisbon group was unaware of the situation in Sicily and ordered the Savoia Marchetti to take off immediately for Rome. He was incensed when OC 2864 Squadron, who had been sworn to secrecy by the C-in-C's staff, would not divulge his reasons for refusing to comply with the direct orders of a senior officer. A furious confrontation ensued, with senior officers of the USAAF supporting the British officer's demand, but Squadron Leader Langham and his armed sentries would not give way, despite threats of arrest and court-martial from all sides. After several hours of an increasingly tense stand-off, the situation was resolved by the appearance of a fleet of staff cars carrying Field Marshal Alexander and the Italian delegation, who then joined their compatriots in the Italian transport aircraft for their return to Italy, leaving a very relieved Squadron Leader Langham to be congratulated by the head of the Allied Military Government in Sicily, Major-General Lord Rennell of Rodd, on carrying out his orders in the face of extreme provocation by senior officers who were unaware of the real situation.

*The Savoia Marchetti aircraft which landed at Palermo in August 1943 with Italian emissaries to negotiate an armistice.* (A Langham)

## THE ITALIAN CAMPAIGN

The first Allied forces crossed the Straits of Messina and landed in mainland Italy on 3 September 1943. Within a fortnight Nos. 2862, 2859 and 2925 LAA Squadrons were flown to Taranto to defend the airfields at Grottalie and Giola del Colle. They were followed to Italy by 2856, 2855, 2857, 2904 and 2858 Squadrons, all of which moved by road, after crossing the Straits of Messina, to the Bari-Taranto area on the east coast of Italy. Under the control of a wing HQ commanded by Lieutenant Colonel Bowdery of Middle East Command, they provided low-level air defence for the complex of airfields in the Foggia plain, from which the majority of bomber sorties were mounted against targets in north Italy, Austria and the Balkans. Meanwhile Nos.2906, 2859, 2860, 2865 and 2867 Squadrons were deployed to airfields in the Naples area on the west coast before redeploying further north to Vasto as the Allied forces advanced.

At the end of 1943 the RAF Regiment force level in Italy totalled twenty squadrons: thirteen LAA and seven field. Elsewhere in the Mediterranean 2864 Squadron remained at Palermo in Sicily, 2869 Squadron was at Sassari in Sardinia, 2866 Squadron was deployed at Bastia in Corsica and 2934 Squadron was retained in Malta. However, with the declining enemy air threat in Italy and the preparations for the forthcoming invasion of North-West Europe, the Regiment strength in the Central Mediterranean and the Middle East was reviewed by the Air Ministry which ordered it to be reduced to a total of 8,500 officers and airmen from 1 January 1944. Accordingly, six LAA squadrons (2861, 2862, 2863, 2865, 2868 and 2869) were transferred to the United Kingdom in the first half of 1944 and a further six squadrons (2855, 2870, 2904, 2906, 2925 and 2934) were later disbanded and their personnel returned to the UK. At the same time the remaining seven squadrons in North Africa (2721, 2744, 2771, 2788, 2825 Field and 2866 and 2905 LAA) were deployed to Italy to fill the gap.

This left five field and fifteen LAA squadrons in Italy and AVM J. M. Robb confirmed the Regiment's *raison d'être* by issuing Command policy for the field squadrons to defend forward airfields against ground attack and airfields in the rear areas against airborne attack. In an advance the field squadrons were to seize enemy airfields for RAF use and in a withdrawal they were to defend RAF airfields until aircraft and equipment had been evacuated. The LAA squadrons were to defend airfields and radar installations within the tactical area (the Italian mainland, Sicily and islands in the Tyrrhenian and Adriatic Seas) against air attack.

Accordingly all five field squadrons, and nine of the LAA squadrons, were deployed on the Italian mainland while the remaining six LAA squadrons were assigned to Sicily, Sardinia, Corsica and off-shore islands used by the RAF. The fourteen squadrons deployed in Italy were then grouped into three wings, 1319, 1320 and 1321, which were all under Colonel Salmon's control , for operational and administrative purposes.

In January 1944 "A" Flight of 2867 LAA Squadron was detached to the island of Ponza, west of Naples, to protect an RAF radar station which had been established there. During a storm in February an American LST (Landing Ship Tank) en route from Anzio to Naples with one hundred and fifty American officers and enlisted men and fifty German prisoners of war on board was driven onto the rocks at the foot of the high cliff on which the radar equipment was sited. Flight Lieutenant Purser, Sergeant Overend and LAC Caton, all of 2867 Squadron, together with Flying Officer Goddard of the radar unit, climbed down the precipitous cliff face and began the task of rescuing survivors under the direction of Flight Lieutenant Purser. Without waiting for the other Regiment and RAF personnel who were making their way to the scene of the wreck, Flying Officer Goddard, Sergeant Overend and LAC Caton began pulling survivors ashore and plunged into the sea to rescue others. During an attempt to save a German POW, Flying Officer Goddard was swept away in the mountainous seas and drowned. In an operation lasting five hours, more than 160 of the 200 Americans and Germans on board the LST were rescued and the US Army recognized the gallantry of Sergeant Overend and LAC Caton by awarding them each the Soldier's Medal, the American equivalent of the George Medal. Flight Lieutenant Purser and five other members of 2867 Squadron received AOC-in-C's Commendations for their actions in this incident.

In April 1944 Nos.2771 and 2788 Field Squadrons, wearing the shoulder flash of the American 5th Army, were deployed in the British front line north of Cassino. Under the command of a New Zealand brigade they held positions at the end of the winding track leading to the precipitous Belvedere Heights for most of the time. However, in May 1944 the Regiment squadrons were temporarily redeployed to reinforce the line between the Black Watch and the Royal Fusiliers on the high ground to the north of the aptly-named Inferno Bowl.

Here the squadrons were engaged in patrolling and harassing enemy positions with medium mortar fire. The enemy-held position known as Point 708 was a particular feature of this activity and attracted daily fire tasks of between fifty and two hundred and fifty 3″ mortar bombs from the support flights of the two Regiment squadrons. After one particularly heavy bombardment the German defences were set on fire

*Major-General CF Liardet CB DSO, Colonel HM Salmon MC and officers of 2788 Field Squadron at Cassino in February 1944.* (N. Salmon)

*OC 2771 Sqn and Colonel Salmon at Cassino.* (N. Salmon)

and the screams of the enemy wounded drifted across the valley until German ambulances flying red cross flags appeared, and the Regiment mortars fell silent.

It was not a comfortable time for the squadrons as the daylight hours had to be spent in bunkers or trenches, especially in the forward defended localities where the sections could not leave their positions without attracting Spandau fire from Point 708. The hours of darkness were taken up with resupply tasks, improving fire positions, and patrolling in no-man's-land where encounters with enemy patrols were not uncommon. Both squadrons were commended by the British and New Zealand divisional commanders for their successes in action against the enemy.

The preparations for the invasion of France increased the need for more LAA squadrons in 2nd Tactical Air Force, which would control RAF operations in North-West Europe, and this led to further reductions in the number of LAA squadrons in the Mediterranean from fifteen to eight. However, three LAA squadrons (2900, 2913

*2771 Sqn mortar position at Cassino.* (N Salmon)

*Sqn Ldr Langham and Flt Lt Gibbs of 2864 Sqn in Italy 1944.* (AC Langham)

& 2916) from the Middle East were sent to Italy as replacements in May 1944, when they were especially welcome as they were already equipped with 40mm Bofors guns. Within three months they were followed by the remaining squadrons in the Middle East (2907, 2908, 2914, 2923, 2924, 2926, 2932 & 2933), which denuded the Middle East Command of all its Regiment units.

Squadron Leader Richard Cox's 2933 LAA Squadron was deployed at Tortorella in August 1943 when a USAAF P38 Lightning taking off on a test flight crashed into the squadron's tented headquarters, where most of the squadron had assembled following a cricket match . In the resulting fireball eight airmen were killed outright and another nine, of whom seven died later, were seriously injured. Regiment officers and airmen, as well as USAAF personnel, showed great courage in going into the inferno to rescue their comrades and Corporal Stevens (the squadron cook), LACs Pike and Gibson, all of 2933 Squadron, and Corporal Ruellis, USAAF, were commended by the AOC-in-C for their gallantry.

After the Allied landings at Anzio another "S" force was assembled to enter Rome and obtain vital intelligence information ahead of the main body of the army. Nos.2721 and 2788 Field Squadrons were selected as the escort force and placed under command of the US 5th Army for the

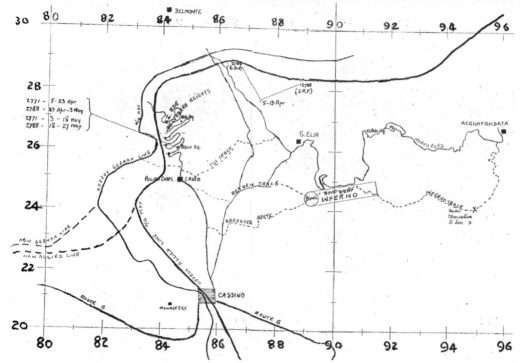

*Sketch map showing RAF Regiment Squadron locations near Cassino in April/May 1944.*
(N Salmon)

operation. 2721 Squadron, already in action with 5th Army in the Anzio salient, escorted the USAAF technical intelligence team which was to enter Italian Air Force bases ahead of the advancing 5th Army to secure secret enemy documents and equipment. The squadron which seized Ciampino airfield, ten miles south of Rome, was the first Allied unit into Ostia and Fiumicino and entered Rome with the leading American troops on 6 June 1944. At Guidona the squadron found the prototype Caproni jet aircraft as well as a new Cant bomber and a large stock of glider bombs. Squadron Leader McMichael, the commander of 2721 Squadron, was awarded the American Bronze Star in recognition of his squadron's contribution to the success of the USAAF mission.

2906 Field Squadron had landed at Salerno in September before moving to Monte Corvino to link up with an Intelligence group and escort it to the airfield at Capodochino to recover enemy equipment under hostile bombardment. From there the squadron's armoured flight raced ahead to seize Capua airfield as the enemy withdrew. When that task was complete, the squadron redeployed to Foggia before being employed in the Ground/Air Landmark role in support of the advance on the east coast of Italy.

2788 Field Squadron had been held in reserve for the Rome operation and in the following month it was assigned to Operation *Anvil*, the invasion of southern France, and landed on the beaches at St

*Italian 20mm Breda AA gun used by 2864 Sqn* (AC Langham)

Raphael, betweeen Cannes and St Tropez as part of 324 Group RAF. The requirement for the inclusion of 2788 Squadron in the operation was to carry out an intelligence-gathering role in occupying what the Air Staff believed would be abandoned enemy airfields at Ramatouelle, Sisteron and Valence; the possibility of any enemy presence, let alone opposition, at these objectives was not even considered by the staff officers concerned. This misconceived appreciation required the squadron to be broken into sub-units which were then committed independently to each airfield. The result was that detachments, too small for effective action against an enemy, were sent forward, unsupported, without any prior reconnaissance or intelligence information. As it happened, two of the airfields, Ramatouelle on the coast to the west of St Tropez, and Sisteron in the mountains 100 kms inland, were taken without incident as the Germans had already abandoned them and withdrawn northwards.

The major airfield at Valence, 200 kms from the coast, in the Rhone valley between Avignon and Lyon, was the next RAF objective and the

"COMMENDATION.

THE COMMANDER-IN-CHIEF, ROYAL AIR FORCE, MEDITERRANEAN AND MIDDLE EAST, WISHES TO BRING TO THE NOTICE OF ALL RANKS THE COURAGE AND DEVOTION TO DUTY DISPLAYED BY THE UNDERMENTIONED AIRMEN AND DIRECTS THAT AN ANNOTATION BE MADE ON THEIR DOCUMENTS ACCORDINGLY.

| | | | |
|---|---|---|---|
| 1103614 | Cpl. Stevens, H.M. | - | 2933 Sqdn. R.A.F. Regt. |
| 1006143 | LAC. Pike, T. | - | 2933 Sqdn. R.A.F. Regt. |
| 1107767 | LAC. Gibson, H. | - | 2933 Sqdn. R.A.F. Regt. |
| 32529427 | Cpl. Ruellius G.A. | - | 368 Servicing Sqdn., 324th. Servicing Group, XVth U.S.A.A.F. |

When a Lightning aircraft recently crashed into the airmen's tented lines at an airfield in Italy, there was a large explosion and an enormous sheet of flame enveloped the area in which the tents were situated.

Cpl. Stevens saw an airman - Cpl. Parkinson - moving in one of the blazing tents and with Cpl. George Ruellius of 368th Servicing Squadron, U.S.A.A.F., a neighbouring unit, dashed into the fire to assist Cpl. Parkinson away from the flames. By this time a considerable amount of ammunition was exploding and Cpl. Ruellius was hit in the shoulder and had to retire before Cpl. Parkinson could be got out of the fire.

Seeing that Cpl. Stevens was not able to save Cpl. Parkinson single handed and in spite of exploding ammunition and the fact that Cpl. Ruellius had already been hit, LAC. Gibson entered the area of the blaze and assisted Cpl. Stevens to drag Cpl. Parkinson who was saturated with burning petrol away from the crash. Cpl. Stevens and LAC. Gibson rolled Cpl. Parkinson in a blanket to extinguish the flames and then assisted in the fire fighting.

LAC. Pike was within 10 yards of the aircraft when it crashed and suffered burns on the arms and legs, but when an airman soaked in burning petrol dashed out of the fire in a hysterical condition, with no thought of personal safety and in spite of his own injuries, LAC. Pike tackled this airman and rolled him on the ground in a piece of canvas and extinguished the flames. After this he helped with the fire fighting and only when the blaze was under control would he go to the Sick Bay for attention.

Unfortunately, both the rescued men died later in hospital from their injuries.

The above mentioned airmen showed great presence of mind and personal courage and their prompt and unselfish actions have set a very high standard to their comrades."

*Commendation by AOC-in-C, RAF Mediterranean and Middle East, for personnel involved in the incident at Tortorella in August 1943.* (N Salmon)

Group HQ staff all too readily assumed that the same situation existed there. Accordingly, Flying Officer Mead of 2788 Squadron, with a token force of two armoured cars and a dozen men in a soft-skinned truck, was ordered to travel northwards up the Rhone valley along Route Nationale 7 towards the town of Valence and occupy the adjacent airfield.

To Mead's surprise his party encountered the forward elements of the US Army engaged in contesting a German counter-attack some distance south of Valence. No one knew if the airfield was still in German occupation or not and the American commander advised the Regiment group to make a circular approach from the east, via Mallemort and Crest, to the airfield. Having liberated the town of Mallemort on the way, the three vehicles were advancing along the road from Crest to Chabeuil when they ran into a company-strength road block which turned out to be the rearguard of a retreating German column. A sharp fire fight ensued, during which the outnumbered and outgunned Regiment force suffered casualties, with both of its armoured cars being knocked out by 20mm fire, before being surrounded and captured. However, Mead and most of his men subsequently escaped from the train in which they were being taken to Germany and rejoined their squadron within a few days.

Meanwhile in Italy the provision of close support to the Army by USAAF and RAF bomber aircraft was causing problems. The uncertainty of the forward postions of the ground forces, coupled with the problems of target identification, had reduced the effectiveness of the air effort and a solution was urgently required if the momentum of the Allied advance was to be sustained. The joint army and air staff answer was to develop the improvised system of Ground/Air Landmarks which had been devised in the Western Desert campaign into a rather more sophisticated structure. With the much greater resources which were available in Italy, this would provide identification points from which routes to the target area would be marked, leading to visual indication points from which the aircrew could accurately determine the position of friendly troops and the direction and distance to the designated target area. These landmarks had to be set up at short notice, by day and night, and moved rapidly as the land battle changed: on occasions as many as six different GALs had to be laid out within 24 hours by a single squadron. The units carrying out these tasks had to have good mobility and map reading skills, excellent radio communications and the ability to operate in small, self-contained, sub-units, requirements which fitted the RAF Regiment squadron organization, and Nos.2856, 2866, 2867, 2744 and 2906 Squadrons were all employed at various times in this way from 1944 until the war ended.

The sheer size of these tasks was illustrated by the GALs laid by 2744 Field Squadron in March 1945 prior to the assault crossing of the River Senio between Ravenna and Bologna in northern Italy. The stores required to mark the GALs for this single operation included 36,000 yards of one-yard-wide white calico, 31,000 yellow smoke generators,

80

*2864 Squadron Guard of Honour for Air Marshal JC Slessor – September 1943.* (N Salmon)

200 fluorescent panels and eight large smoke-generating vehicles and trailers. Ground markers had to be set out from the point at which the bombers were to cross the coast to the river crossings 20 miles inland. The forward positions of the 8th Army were marked by white Ts, each measuring 50 yards by 15 yards, set out 1,000 yards apart along a 9-mile frontage, to ensure that bombs were not dropped on friendly forces. All this had to be done by two field flights at first light on the day of the attack, so as not to give the enemy advance warning of the planned operation. Similar GALs were often set out for night attacks, using flares instead of calico markers and smoke indicators. In all such operations the critical ground markers had to be set out close to the front line, an area which was normally well within enemy artillery and mortar range and where routine harassing fire by the enemy posed a threat to troops necessarily working in the open without any form of cover. 2744 Squadron particularly distinguished itself in these operations and Flying Officer Ringer and Corporal Hope were awarded the MC and MM respectively for their actions under enemy fire while setting out GALs for the Army.

The Germans soon came to realize the contribution which the GALs close to the front line made to the accuracy of the air attacks on their positions. In an effort to counter the activities of the GAL units, the enemy often tried to infiltrate patrols through the Allied forward positions in the hope of ambushing GAL parties and disrupting the RAF and USAAF air support operations.

In September 1944 a 2744 Squadron reconnaissance team consisting of Flying Officer Harris, Corporal Hadley and LAC Watt drove their jeep towards the small Italian village of Stradone to select a suitable GAL site. As it happened, the village was occupied by a German patrol which had worked its way through the forward British positions and was waiting for a suitable target to appear. The first burst of enemy fire brought the jeep

81

*Ground-to-Air Landmarks showing the route from the Adriatic coast to the front line in Italy for RAF and USAAF bomber aircraft in 1945.* (N. Salmon)

to a sudden stop and the occupants dived for cover and managed to reach a nearby barn in which they found four British soldiers, also sheltering from enemy fire. Having returned the enemy fire, Harris led the party out of the building into dead ground to reach a better fire position from which to engage the enemy. While the group was in the open they came under a barrage of fire from light mortars and all were wounded by the blast and fragmentation of the exploding mortar bombs. Despite a serious chest wound, Flying Officer Harris crawled forward to recover the jeep and brought it back to collect the wounded men. Loading them in the vehicle, he drove four miles down a rough track to an Army field dressing station before collapsing from loss of blood. He was subsequently awarded the Military Cross for his gallantry in action.

The Regiment's interaction in ground/air support operations was complemented by using the armoured car flights of the field squadrons to link the forward elements of army units to the ground attack aircraft providing their close air support. An example of the effectiveness of the Regiment in this role occurred one morning in late 1944 when the leading battalion of a New Zealand brigade, which was advancing northwards from Rimini, was held up by a German strongpoint south of Bellaria. The corporal commanding the attached 2744 Squadron armoured car called for air support and gave the target indication to the aircraft "cab rank" overhead. A very effective air strike was delivered almost immediately on the enemy position and the New Zealanders' advance continued with less than ten minutes delay. This was only one example of a successful and sustained use of RAF Regiment expertise, mobility and communications in directing RAF fighter-bomber aircraft against opposition encountered by the Army as the German forces were steadily driven northwards towards the Austrian border.

In September 1944 HQ 8th Army appealed to the AOC-in-C for the loan of field squadrons of the RAF Regiment to overcome the Army's shortage of infantry in the advance towards the Gothic Line, the German defences which ran from Pisa to Rimini. 2721 Squadron was immediately placed under command of X Corps and assigned to provide the close infantry support to the armoured car regiments in the van of the British advance northwards. Arriving at San Angelo, the squadron was attached to the King's Dragoon Guards, which was shortly afterwards replaced by the Household Cavalry Regiment. In October 2721 Squadron was at Alfero, attached to the Lovat Scouts whose colonel had to ask them to reduce their aggressive patrolling as this was causing the enemy to reinforce the sector in anticipation of a major attack. In November the squadron was supporting Skinner's Horse of the Indian Army before joining the 27th Lancers at Essico Ioriso, with whom they attacked and captured the German strongpoint in the village of Fosso di Ghiaia on the River Savio. While the river was being bridged by the Royal Engineers, the squadron positions were subjected to intensive enemy artillery bombardments in which several Regiment casualties were sustained.

At dawn on 19 November, again with the 27th Lancers, 2721 Squadron launched an attack on the next village, Classe Fuori, where the key to the enemy defences was a large sugar factory. The fire support for the assault was impressive and ranged from 5.5″ medium artillery, through 25-pounder self-propelled guns and 75mm howitzers to the .50″ machine guns of Popski's Private Army which was operating with the local Italian partisan group on the flanks of the main axis. 2721 Squadron stormed the sugar factory, suffering only one casualty, LAC Stratton, who received fatal shrapnel wounds, and found that the prisoners they took were from the Wehrmacht's 721 Jaeger Regiment, almost their numerical opposite numbers.

A period of artillery duels and intensive patrolling by both sides resulted in a series of small-scale engagements, including one in which a German fighting patrol attacked the reserve flight of 2721 Squadron with anti-tank rocket launchers. Flying Officer McNally promptly shot the enemy patrol commander with his pistol, and the Germans abandoned their weapons and fled.

On 28 November 2721 Squadron and the 27th Lancers continued their advance, forcing the crossing of the River Uniti and entering Ravenna ahead of 5 Canadian Armoured Brigade whose leading unit,

*Arrival of Commandant RAF Regiment in Naples in March 1944. L to R: Maj-Gen Liardet, Col Salmon, Flt Lt Tye, Fg Off O'Sullivan.* (N Salmon)

Princess Louise's Dragoon Guards, was disconcerted to find the British already in occupation. When Colonel Salmon visited the 27th Lancers their commanding officer, Lieutenant-Colonel Horsbrugh-Porter DSO, expressed his gratitude for the support he had received from 2721 Squadron, saying that the squadron's initiative, competence and reliability were second to none and he wished that other such experienced and seasoned troops from the RAF Regiment could be made available to support his regiment on a regular basis.

From Ravenna onwards 2721 Squadron came under command of the Canadian brigade and was attached to Lord Strathcona's Horse for the advance to the River Lamone where a British brigade took over once more and 2721 Squadron was placed in support of another British cavalry regiment, the 7th Hussars. At this point General McCreery, the GOC-in-C 8th Army and Major-General Hull, the GOC 1st Armoured Division, visited the squadron to congratulate the officers and airmen on their outstanding performance while operating with armoured regiments of the Army. In December 1944, following an advance of 100 kms and three months in the front line, 2721 Squadron was relieved by 2788 Squadron, which had returned to Italy from the south of France. The OC 2721 Squadron, Squadron Leader Norman McMichael, was subsequently awarded the Military Cross in recognition of his leadership and his squadron's achievements in intensive operations against the enemy. The gallantry of Corporal A. G. Bradfield at Classe Fuori and in subsequent actions leading to the crossing of the River Uniti was recognized by the award of the Military Medal. Corporal P. L. A. Short also received the Military Medal in a subsequent list of honours and awards.

2788 Squadron was with the Hussars, and the Lancers, for the capture of Fusignano and the subsequent advance to the River Po in January 1945. But by March 1945 there were more pressing tasks for the Regiment elsewhere and 2788 was withdrawn from Italy and redeployed to Palestine to counter the internal security threat to RAF installations there.

## THE BALKANS

Headquarters Balkan Air Force was established at Bari, on the east coast of Italy, to control air operations in the Adriatic, Greece and the Balkans and to provide air support for HQ Land Forces Adriatic in their operations against German forces in those areas. In June 1944 HQ 1321 Wing, with 2825 Field and 2923 and 2926 LAA Squadrons, was placed under command of Balkan Air Force at Altamura from where the two LAA squadrons were redeployed to Canne and Biferno on the Adriatic coast.

At that time the Germans held all the islands off the Dalmatian coast except for Vis and Lagosta. The Yugoslav partisan commander Josip Broz, or Tito as he called himself, had fortified Vis as his alternative headquarters in case he was forced to leave the mainland. As there was a short airstrip on the island, which could be used for forward fighter operations, a flight of 2867 LAA Squadron was detached to HQ BAF and deployed to Vis to defend the airstrip with its 20mm Hispanos until it could be replaced by Squadron Leader Donald Pocock's 2932 LAA Squadron with its 40mm Bofors guns.

2825 Field Squadron then deployed to Vis to undergo intensive commando training preparation alongside 2932 Squadron before both squadrons joined Land Forces Adriatic in numerous amphibious

```
                        COPY.

To: MAAF  (R) AFHQ
From:  BALKAN AIR FORCE
                              BAF/143     JULY 15
UNDERSTAND THAT 3 FIELD SQUADRONS (R) FIELD SQUADRONS RAF REGT NOW IN
MIDDLE EAST MIGHT BECOME AVAILABLE FOR RE-ALLOCATION.  THESE WOULD BE
MOST VALUABLE ADDITION TO LAND FORCES ADRIATIC WHOSE LIMITED RESOURCES
WILL HINDER OUR TRANS-ADRIATIC OPERATIONS FROM AUGUST ONWARDS.  PROPOSE
THAT THESE SQUADRONS SHOULD BE USED INITIALLY TO REPLACE COMMANDOS WITHDRAWN
FROM VIS FOR RAIDS AND WOULD THEN GRADUALLY INTRODUCE THEM TO OFFENSIVE
OPERATIONS UNDER LAND FORCES ADRIATIC.     TOO 151145B


To: HQ RAF ME (R)  AFHQ   BAF
From:  HQ MAAF
                        JCS.232     JULY 16      SECRET
A.O.C. BALKAN AIR FORCE IS ANXIOUS TO OBTAIN THE SERVICES OF THE THREE
FIELD SQUADRONS OF THE R.A.F.REGIMENT NOW IN THE LEVANT FOR SERVICE IN
THE ADRIATIC.  THEY WOULD BE USED INITIALLY TO GARRISON VIS THUS RELEASING
COMMANDOS AND OTHER TROOPS FOR OFFENSIVE RAIDING OPERATIONS UNDER L.F.A.
YOUR VIEWS REQUESTED AS TO WHETHER CONDITIONS IN PALESTINE LIKELY TO BE
SUCH AS TO JUSTIFY WITHDRAWAL OF THESE UNITS HAVING REGARD TO NECESSITY
FOR PROTECTION OF R.A.F. INSTALLATIONS IN EVENT OF TROUBLES.
IMPORTANT.                  (SGD) J.S.ORME, W/Cdr. P.S.O. to
Copy to: Col.Salmon. *              Air Marshal, D. Air C.in C.


To: HQ MAAF
From: HQ RAF MIDDLE EAST
                        AD 196     17 JULY
REF YOUR JCS.232 JULY 16.  DO NOT CONSIDER SITUATION IN PALESTINE JUSTIFIES
THE RETENTION OF THREE FIELD SQUADRONS WHO HAVE BEEN HIGHLY TRAINED FOR
AN OFFENSIVE ROLE.  MORALE OF TROOPS EXCEPTIONALLY HIGH AND WILL DETERIORATE
IF THEY REMAIN INDEFINITELY ON GARRISON DUTIES.  ARMY ASSUME RESPONSIBILITY
FOR GROUND DEFENCE IN EVENT OF TROUBLES ASSISTED BY IRAQ LEVIES AND STATION
PERSONNEL WHERE AVAILABLE.          TOO 171347Z.
DIST: A/M.Slessor
      Col.Salmon


To: AFHQ ALGIERS (R) FAIRBANKS
From:  EAKER
                        18 JULY  TOP SECRET  MX.25037.
REF BALKAN AIR FORCE SIGNAL BAF 143 JULY 15 AND THIS HQRS SIGNAL JCS 232
JULY 16.  AOC-IN-C MIDDLE EAST CONSIDERS THESE FIELD SQUADRONS CAN BE MADE
AVAILABLE.  HE STATES THEY ARE HIGHLY TRAINED AND FIRST CLASS TROOPS WHOSE
MORALE WILL DETERIORATE IF THEY ARE KEPT INDEFINITELY ON GARRISON DUTIES
IN LEVANT.  SUGGEST YOU CONCUR IN PROPOSAL IN BAF 143 SUBJECT TO ANY
REQUIREMENTS IN CONNECTION WITH POSSIBLE DESPATCH OF FORCE TO TURKEY
WHICH WILL BE CLARIFIED WITHIN A FEW DAYS.     TOO 181210B
Dist: D/air C-in-C.  Col.Salmon.
```

*Exchange of signals regarding employment of RAF Regiment squadrons in the Balkan Air Force.* (N Salmon)

*AOC Balkan Air Force inspecting 1321 Wing at Bari with Wing Commander J Simpson and Colonel HM Salmon MC in July 1944.* (N. Salmon)

operations along the coastline with elements of Royal Navy, Royal Marine and Army forces operating as part of Land Forces Adriatic. Small groups were embarked in naval motor torpedo boats and motor gun boats as boarding parties, while larger detachments of flight strength landed on offshore islands and the Yugoslav mainland to support Royal Artillery field guns giving fire support to partisans, as well as reinforcing Royal Marine Commandos in carrying out amphibious assaults. In November 1944 2825 Squadron occupied Dubrovnik as part of a composite force and remained there until January 1945.

Typical of the raiding tasks undertaken by 1321 Wing units was a landing at Cherso. After capturing the sentries, the Regiment force destroyed the Osor bridge and re-embarked without loss. On another occasion two Regiment flights provided the covering force for batteries of the Royal Artillery which landed on Korcula and shelled enemy positions. The Germans responded with heavy and accurate counter-battery fire, which caused casualties to RA and RAF Regiment personnel, before close air support from Hurricane fighter/bombers silenced the enemy guns.

Another Regiment detachment landed on Brac with an RAF signals unit to establish a transmitting station to direct aircraft against ground targets. This continued to operate despite attracting enemy artillery fire which caused some casualties. Other Regiment personnel from 2825 and 2932 Squadrons were regularly embarked as boarding parties in Royal Navy motor gun boats and motor torpedo boats based at Komiza which patrolled the islands and coastline of Yugoslavia to harass German outposts and attack enemy supply vessels. Such actions usually resulted in the enemy ships being left on fire or sinking, but whenever

*AOC Balkan Air Force addressing officers and airmen of 1321 Wing ("Celyforce") at Bari.*
(N Salmon)

possible the Regiment boarding parties took off survivors for interrogation and transfer to Italy as prisoners of war.

The success of the Regiment squadrons in these operations led to a further wing HQ, No.1328, being formed with three field squadrons-2902, 2908 and 2924, under command and assigned to the Balkan Air Force to support the expansion of joint-Service operations in the Adriatic and Ionian Seas. When 2771 Field Squadron was redeployed from Greece to the Balkan Air Force, it was attached to the Royal Artillery's raiding support regiment to provide close protection for the field guns in attacks on the Yugoslav coast. One such operation was an assault on the German-held island of Pag, which lasted for several days, during which heavy casualties were inflicted on the garrison before the squadron withdrew, taking with them over fifty German prisoners.

*AOC Balkan Air Force inspecting the Special Duties Section of 1328 Wing ("Celyforce') at Bari prior to raiding operations on the Jugoslav coast.* (N Salmon)

*Special Order of the Day by FM Sir Harold Alexander, Supreme Commander Mediterranen Theatre, April 1945.*
(N Salmon)

An RAF Regiment parachute force had been formed from 2721 and 2771 Field Squadrons to support RAF air liaison teams which were intended to operate on the Yugoslav mainland. This Special Duties Section later became part of 1328 Wing and was known as Celyforce after its commander, Squadron Leader Cely-Trevilian. Once Tito had refused to allow British forces to operate with his partisans inside Yugoslavia Celyforce lost its airborne role and was attached to the Royal Marine Special Boat Squadron, taking part in a series of cloak and dagger raids on the Yugoslavian coast with the Royal Marines.

In February 1945 1328 Wing, with 2825 Field and 2914 LAA Squadrons under command, landed on the Yugoslav mainland to secure the airfield at Prkos/Zara and develop it as an emergency landing ground for disabled RAF and USAAF bombers returning to their bases in Italy after attacking targets in Austria and Rumania. The return of 2771 Field Squadron from Greece to the Balkan Air Force enabled its armoured

*Armoured cars of 2771 Field Squadron escorting German prisoners of war in Jugoslavia in March 1945.* (IWM-CL.3482)

car flight to be detached to 1328 Wing while the remainder of the squadron was retained in raiding tasks on the Yugoslav coast. With Royal Engineers to maintain the runway, USAAF groundcrews to repair damaged aircraft, 2914 Squadron to provide LAA defence and 2825 Squadron to defend the airfield against ground attack while 2771's armoured cars provided the reconnaissance screen, the airfield operated successfully under the protection of 1328 Wing until VE-Day, when Marshal Tito ordered all Allied forces to leave Yugoslav territory.

*A 40mm Bofors gun detachment of 2914 LAA Squadron on a Hurricane squadron airfield in Jugoslavia in February 1945.* (IWM-CL.3486)

## GREECE

In September 1944 it was decided by HQ BAF to deploy aircraft to southern Greece as a prelude to attacking the German forces which were occupying the country. A task force consisting of detachments of the Special Boat Squadron and the Long Range Desert Group, a troop of Royal Marine Commandos, a company of the Highland Light Infantry, a detachment of Royal Engineers, 2908 Field Squadron, a composite RAF Regiment mine clearance flight from 1321 Wing and an RAF airfield party was assembled at Bari to seize the airfield at Araxos in the Peloponnese. This force of 450 officers and men, under the command of Lieutenant-Colonel Lord Jellicoe, was codenamed *Bucketforce* and sailed from Bari towards Katakolon, south-west of Araxos. A separate group, codenamed *Rowanbucket*, consisted of an RAF operating party and a 1321 Wing composite mineclearing force of two officers and thirty-nine NCOs and aircraftmen drawn from 2902 and 2924 Field Squadrons and 2923 and 2926 LAA Squadrons. Both groups sailed together from Bari on 24 September 1944 in a convoy consisting of a destroyer, a minesweeper and seven landing craft, reaching the Greek port of Katakolon two days later.

A reconnaissance group of 1st SBS dropped by parachute near Araxos on 23 September and, having reported on the state of airfield, the advance party of *Bucketforce* arrived by air the following day. Following an unopposed landing by the main body at the small port of Katakolon, the condition of roads and tracks on the island was so bad that they took a further 20 hours to cover the 40 miles to Araxos. On reaching the airfield, Regiment personnel began the task of clearing mines and making the runway serviceable. The unexpected appearance of a German Ju88 during this preparatory work made it expedient to summon a flight of 2923 LAA Squadron to be flown in to provide anti-aircraft defence for the airfield.

Lord Jellicoe ordered his force to "chase the Hun out of the western Peloponnese" and sent 2908 Squadron's armoured car and support flights to test the defences of Patras on the Gulf of Corinth. Reports from the town revealed that while the German commander there was willing to negotiate a surrender, his subordinate officers refused to obey his orders and insisted on continuing to defend the port and town. The situation was further complicated by the German-oficered Greek security battalion, which was anxious to surrender to the British before the Greek partisan forces arrived to wreak vengeance on them.

After probing attacks against enemy positions by 2908 Squadron and Royal Marine Commandos, the assault on Patras began on 1 October. The Germans were still trying to evacuate their troops by sea and offered fierce resistance in an attempt to protect the harbour and the ships which were still being loaded with men and supplies. After a reconnaissance of the harbour by Flying Officer Horrocks and Sgt Stewart, two of the squadron's 6 pounder anti-tank guns were manhandled along the coast road within sight of the enemy and successfully engaged two German E-Boats in the harbour. After dark, Flying Officer Sacks with a corporal and two ACs entered Patras to reconnoitre the German positions while Fg Off Rust took a fighting patrol to test the strength of the enemy force holding Wireless Hill, which dominated the town. When the fire fight began, 3″ mortar fire was called down on the hill, killing or wounding the crews of the two field guns sited there. Wireless Hill was captured shortly after midnight, making the German positions elsewhere untenable, and the following morning 2908 Squadron made an unopposed entry into Patras, where they received an ecstatic welcome from the civilian population.

*Bucketforce* then continued its advance to the mainland of Greece. 2908 Squadron crossed the Corinth Canal and after another engagement with the retreating German forces at Megalo Pekvo, in which LAC Pete Ward won a Military Medal when he broke up an enemy attack on an SBS position by machine-gunning the attackers from his armoured car and pursuing the survivors until they surrendered, entered Athens with the leading British forces. From there the squadron was divided, one element returning to the Peleponnese to

*Flt Lt Cottle and Sgt Pulham, both of 2926 LAA Squadron, examining German land mines lifted from Araxos airfield by the mine clearing detachment from 1321 Wing RAF Regiment.*
(Crown Copyright/MOD)

assist in the pacification of Sparti, where rival Greek forces were at each other's throats, and the other becoming part of *Pompforce*, which comprised two companies of 4th Parachute Regiment, a detachment of the Special Boat Service and the armoured cars and the 3″ mortars of 2908 Squadron RAF Regiment, which was tasked to pursue the retreating Germans towards the Yugoslavian border. In a fierce action at Kozani, just inside Yugoslavia, one of 2908 Squadron's armoured cars received several hits from German 37mm anti-tank guns, killing the car commander, Flying Officer Dennis. His driver, Corporal Wingate, was wounded but managed to extricate the damaged AFV and reach safety. He was subsequently awarded the Military Medal for his actions.

OC 2908 Squadron was detached, with the main part of his squadron, to Sparti in the southern Peleponnese where a confrontation between Greek communist partisans and a Greek security battalion appeared imminent. Interposing his force between the two parties, Squadron Leader Wynne was able to persuade the partisan commander to restrain his men while the Regiment took the surrender of the thousand-strong security battalion and, after disarming them, placed them in a holding camp on an island connected to the mainland by a causeway, which was secured by 2908 personnel. This did not please the partisans, who had intended to lynch the prisoners, and a difficult situation was contained by a blend of diplomacy and force until boats could be found to transport the surrendered personnel to Piraeus where they became the responsibility of the Greek government forces. Before leaving Sparti, the squadron found an Australian soldier who had been hiding in the hills for three years and took him back to Athens with them.

Also in the theatre at this time, although not part of the RAF Regiment, was No.1 (Parachute) Company of the RAF Levies (Iraq). The Levies were originally a locally-enlisted force of about 1,500 men, under RAF command, which was used between the wars to assist the Air Force in controlling the mandated territory of Iraq. During the Second World War the Iraq Levies were expanded to a strength of 12,000 men in 80 infantry companies, some of which were deployed outside Iraq to defend RAF bases in the Levant.

Land Forces Adriatic mounted an operation against the Albanian port of Sarande, opposite Corfu, in October 1944 to deprive the enemy of the use of the harbour and so prevent the evacuation of German troops by sea. The key feature was a prominent hill dominating the approaches to the port and the parachute company of the Iraq Levies was tasked to seize and hold it so that the Royal Marines could occupy the port itself. The Levies were recruited from the Kurdish and Assyrian tribes which lived in the mountains of northern Iraq and an attack against an enemy-held hilltop feature was an everyday task for them.

Storming up the steep slopes at breakneck speed, they surprised the garrison of a German infantry company, who were still at breakfast, and took the strongpoint without suffering any casualties. Unfortunately, the rapidity of their assault was such that neither the Royal Navy nor the Royal Air Force realized that the objective had been captured so soon after H-Hour and the Levies were subjected to shellfire from naval vessels and rocket attacks from aircraft before it was appreciated that the Germans no longer held the vital ground. Once the Royal Marines knew that the hill was in friendly hands, the port of Sarande was captured without difficulty and the parachute company was moved to Greece to operate alongside the RAF Regiment squadrons which were deployed there.

When the British liberated Greece, the Greek communist party (EAM) attempted to seize power by using its military wing (ELAS) to oppose the return of the Greek government which had been in exile during the war. In December 1944 open warfare broke out between ELAS and the British forces supporting the legitimate Greek government which had returned to Greece. Most of the fighting took place in and around Athens where six RAF Regiment squadrons, and No.1 Company of the Iraq Levies, were deployed. 2771, 2778 and 2926 Squadrons were at Hassani airfield, south-east of Athens, 2908 Squadron was further south at Glifadha, 2902 Squadron was at the port of Piraeus and HQ 1321 Wing and 2923 Squadron were at Kifissia, north-east of Athens, where Air Headquarters Greece was situated. The parachute company of the Iraq Levies was co-located with the Regiment squadrons at Hassani.

The fighting was confused, partly because of the difficulty of identifying the enemy who did not wear distinguishing uniforms and who

*Armoured cars of 2908 and 2771 Field Squadrons patrolling in Athens – 1944.* (Crown
Copyright/MOD)

had no compunction in using women and children to shield their movements and partly because of the ease with which the communist partisans moved among the civilian population. Despite these difficulties, the port installations at Pireaus and the airfield at Hassani were successfully defended; the problem was to be at the Air Headquarters in the pleasant suburb of Kifissia with its well-laid-out streets and comfortable hotels. Chosen as the ideal setting for an RAF Headquarters well before there was any intimation of civil war which would involve the British, it was difficult enough to defend it against infiltration by saboteurs, let alone a serious attack by battle-hardened partisan groups.

When 1321 Wing HQ was deployed to Kifissia, Wing Commander Simpson warned his superiors that the AHQ complex was extremely vulnerable to ground attack and should be moved to a more defensible location, but the only reaction by the Air Staff was to redeploy 2923 LAA Squadron to Kifissia and draft a hundred airmen of assorted ground trades from the Middle East to increase the manpower available for defence. Unfortunately, this was not sufficient to compensate for the inflexibility of improvised defences in a suburban area in the face of a heavily armed and numerically superior enemy force. The anti-aircraft guns of 2923 Squadron were all but useless in the ground role in a built-up area where their detachments were vulnerable to close-range small arms fire, and the majority of the 400 officers and airmen on the headquarters staff had never fired their personal weapons in anger. On 18 December over 1,000 ELAS partisans, supported by artillery and mortars, launched a furious assault on the HQ buildings where the defenders held out for over 48 hours at a cost of eleven killed and forty-six wounded. When news of the action first reached Athens, it was assumed that the attack was a small-scale one and reinforcements would not be required. When the extent of the attack was realized by the Army headquarters in Athens, a relief column headed by heavy armour from the Royal Tank Regiment together with 2926 Squadron and the armoured car flights of 2908 and 2771 Squadrons promptly set out from Hassani. Delayed on route by roadblocks, demolished bridges and mines, the relief column did not arrive in Kifissia until four hours after the last defenders had exhausted their ammunition and had been overwhelmed by the partisans. The survivors were rapidly spirited away into captivity in the mountains where they were subjected to hardship and deliberate ill-treatment by their captors before being released when the ELAS commanders throughout Greece surrendered some weeks later.

Athens was cleared of partisans after several days of street fighting, in which 2902, 2908 and 2771 Squadrons operated under command of 139 Infantry Brigade. The field squadrons' 6 pounder anti-tank guns proved particularly useful in dealing with ELAS strongpoints and snipers operating from buildings. Once peace had been restored, Flying Officer Winfield of 2902 Squadron witnessed the opening of mass graves near Athens. These contained the bodies of hundreds of men, women and children, who had been killed by shooting, stabbing or beating by the ELAS partisans, simply because they had refused to support the communist regime. Sadly, there was no such thing as a war crimes commission to obtain justice for the innocents who had been so ruthlessly and brutally murdered by their compatriots.

In March 1945 all the Regiment squadrons , except 2908 which was retained in Athens, were withdrawn to Italy, from where 1320 and 1328 Wings, with a total of seven squadrons under command, were redeployed to Austria and stationed at Klagenfurt and Moderndorf as part of the occupation forces. That happy state of affairs did not last and it was not long before Regiment wings and squadrons were withdrawn from Italy and Austria to return to the Middle East to reinforce the increasingly inadequate security forces in Palestine where attacks on RAF installations began in January 1946. The rifle squadrons in Palestine were overstretched in being tasked to defend every type of RAF installation, despite being always understrength and grievously short of experienced officers and NCOs. By the end of that year only four squadrons had sufficient manpower to give them any operational capability at all and with too few resources and too many commitments, the ground defence of RAF airfields, supply depots, signals units and headquarters in Palestine became an impossible task for the undermanned Regiment squadrons.

## THE MEDITERRANEAN CAMPAIGN IN RETROSPECT

The North African campaign, and its sequels in the Central Mediterranean theatre, provided the Regiment with its first experience of expeditionary warfare and demonstrated the contribution which staff work makes to operational effectiveness.

As in North Africa, the RAF Regiment staff establishment in the Central Mediterranean consisted of one group captain post, filled by a colonel who was for much of the time in the field in his self-appointed role of 'Commander RAF Regiment', with one junior staff officer, a clerk and a driver. This remarkably economical establishment only worked as well as it did because of Colonel Salmon's personality, leadership and tactical ability, but the lack of day-to-day contact with other branches of the headquarters staff tended to isolate the Regiment from air operations in the theatre. The result was that the air campaign was conducted by RAF officers who were not fully aware of the proper

96

*Colonel HM Salmon CBE MC and Squadron Leader NF McMichael MC in Italy 1945.*
(N Salmon)

roles and capabilities of the Regiment in support of air operations. Despite the close relationship which Salmon always sought to establish with senior RAF officers, there was a recurring tendency for the Air Staff to ignore the structure of Regiment units and specify the number of individual men, vehicles and weapons required for specific operations. Whenever Colonel Salmon became aware of such instructions, his blunt response to more senior RAF officers was to tell them that their function was to state the operational requirement and his to select the Regiment forces which would carry out the task.

The pressure on the Air Ministry to transfer RAF Regiment NCOs and airmen to the Army and the need to add more Regiment squadrons to 2TAF in NW Europe drew manpower away from the Mediterranean and Colonel Salmon had to juggle his resources to maintain an adequate force level. There were innovations and diversions as well: parachute training for a special duties force commanded by Squadron Leader Cely-Trevilian, attachment of Balkan Air Force squadrons to the raiding units of Land Forces Adriatic and the employment of field and LAA squadrons in the counter-insurgency role against the Communist attempt to overthrow the legitimate Greek government after the liberation of Greece.

COPY.

Main Headquarters,
8th ARMY,
Ref: GA/MISC/11
12 July 45.

Air Officer Commanding,
Desert Air Force.

1.     I should like to express my appreciation of the work done by the Armoured Car Section of 2744 Field Squadron, R.A.F. Regiment, whilst employed as part of the Air Support Communication of EIGHTH ARMY.

2.     For more than one year these cars were deployed with leading Brigades which participated in every attack from AREZZO until the final surrender in ITALY.  They formed a vital link in providing radio communication from these Brigades to the ROVER or F.A.C.P. in support, and not once, in spite of hazardous situations and casualties, did they fail in their task.

3.     The untiring efforts and the devotion to duty of the crews manning these cars contributed greatly to the success achieved in providing close air support to the forward troops.  Their record of service is one of which the Squadron and the Regiment may be justly proud.

(signed) R.L. McCREERY,
Lieut-General,
GOC EIGHTH ARMY.

*Message from GOC 8th Army to AOC Desert Air Force – July 1945.* (N Salmon)

That the Regiment's achievements were beginning to be understood and appreciated was reflected in congratulatory messages sent to the Commander RAF Regiment by the AOC-in-C (Air Marshal Sir John Slessor) and the AOC Desert Air Force (AVM R. M. Foster) at Christmas 1944. AVM Foster's signal read: "My best wishes for

*Major-General AE Robinson DSO, who succeeded Major-General Sir Claude Liardet KBE CB DSO as Commandant RAF Regiment, inspecting the RAF Regiment Special Duties Section of 1328 Wing at Klagenfurt in Austria in 1945. Note that, unlike 2810 Parachute Squadron in ACSEA, these personnel wear their parachute badges on the right sleeve.* (IWM-CNA.3722)

Christmas and the New Year. You have done, and are doing, fine work for which the GOC 8th Army has given me his personal thanks. It is a great satisfaction to all of us to know that the RAF is doing its stuff on land just as well as it does it in the air."

## TAILPIECE

Towards the end of the war the AOC-in-C recommended that Colonel Salmon should be appointed CBE in recognition of his outstanding service in the theatre. When the recommendation reached the Air Ministry, Colonel Salmon's name was forwarded to the War Office for inclusion in the Army's list on the grounds that he was an Army officer who was only temporarily serving with the RAF. The War Office promptly downgraded the award from CBE to OBE and when the news of this reached Italy, Colonel Salmon, supported by the AOC-in-C and his staff officers, declined to accept the lower award both on the grounds that several of his own officers had already received that decoration on his recommendation and that all previous awards of the Order of the British Empire to officers of his equivalent rank in the RAF had been at Commander, and not Officer, level.

There were, in the Desert Air Force contingent in Italy at that time, a number of South African Air Force wings and squadrons and the SAAF used army ranks for its personnel. After discussing the problem with the Allied Commander-in-Chief, Field Marshal Sir Harold Alexander, the AOC-in-C ordered his staff to resubmit Colonel Salmon's name, with the suffix "SAAF", for the award of the CBE, knowing that this would ensure that it was dealt with by the Air Ministry and not the War Office.

Two months later Colonel Salmon met Field Marshal Alexander coming out of his headquarters at Caserta. The Commander-in-Chief stopped and said to him, "your CBE will be through any day now", and so it was, even though the *London Gazette* listed the award as being to Colonel H. M. Salmon of the South African Air Force. This was corrected in a subsequent issue of the *Gazette* by noting the deletion of "SAAF" and replacing it by "late Welch Regiment, attached RAF Regiment".

On 14 November 1952, ten years after the *Torch* landings in North Africa, Morrey Salmon hosted a dinner party in London to mark the anniversary. Among his guests were twenty of his wartime RAF Regiment wing commanders and squadron leaders, but also present were Marshal of the RAF Sir John Slessor, Air Chief Marshal Sir James Robb, Major-General Sir Claude Liardet, Air Vice-Marshal Sir Francis Mellersh and Air Vice-Marshal T. C. Traill.

Colonel H. M. Salmon CBE MC★ DL DSc died at his Cardiff home, full of years and honour, on 27 April 1985, aged 93.

## WING HQs IN THE MEDITERRANEAN THEATRE 1944-46

**1319**  Formed Italy March 1944. Trigno-Vasto-San Servero-San Vito-
Pescara – Falconara-Santarcangelo. December 1945 to Palestine.

**1320**  Formed Italy March 1944. Bellavista – Orvieto – Iese – Fano –
Rimini. May 1945 Austria – Klagenfurt. Awards: 1 MID March
1946 to Palestine.

**1321**  Formed Italy April 1944. Foggia – Bari. Balkan Air Force –
Athens – Kifissia. March 1945 to Palestine.

**1322**  From Egypt August 1944. Taranto – Foggia – Naples.
Disbanded November 1944. Awards: 2 MID

**1328**  Formed Italy September 1944. Balkan Air Force. Bari – Prykos
– Zara – Klagenfurt – Meiselburg – Troffiach – Graz.
April 1946 Disbanded. Awards: 1 MID

## SQUADRONS IN THE MEDITERRANEAN THEATRE 1943 – 46

**2721**  **Field** – From North Africa December 1943 – Bagnoli –
Cerignola – Anzio – Rome. October 1944 – Perugia – Citta di
Castello – Rimini – Cesena – Fosso di Ghiaia – Classe Fuori –
Ravenna. Awards: 1 MBE, 1 MC, 5 MMs, 1 US Bronze Star, 17
MID. December 1945 to Palestine.

**2744**  **Field** – From North Africa December 1943 – Naples – Cassino –
Gothic Line. May 1945 – Austria – Zeltweg – Greece –
Glifhada. Awards: 2 OBEs, 1 MBE, 2 MCs, 3 BEM, 2 MMs, 14
MID April 1946 Disbanded.

**2771**  **Field** – From North Africa December 1943 – Naples – Cassino
– Rimini. December 1944 – Land Forces Adriatic – Aegean –
Greece. February 1945 – Yugoslavia – Prykos – Zadar – Austria –
Vienna. Awards: 1 BEM, 8 MID March 1946 – Palestine.

**2788**  **Field** – From North Africa December 1943 – Cassino. July 1944
– Southern France (*Anvil*) – Italy – Ravenna. December 1944 –
Greece – Hassani. Awards: 1 OBE, 1 MBE, 1 MC, 5 MID
March 1945 – Palestine.

**2825**  **Field** – From North Africa December 1943 – Naples –
Amendola – Altamura – Bari. Yugoslavia – Split – Dubrovnik.
Austria – Klagenfurt – Schwechat. Awards: 1 BEM, 5 MID April
1946 Disbanded.

**2855**  **LAA** – From UK July 1943 – (*Husky*) – Sicily – Pachino – Lentini.
Italy – Reggio – Bari – Triolo – Canne – San Marco.
January 1944 Disbanded.

**2856**  **LAA** – From UK July 1943 – (*Husky*) – Sicily – Augusta – Agnone.

Italy – Bari – Foggia – Mileni – Cutella – San Vito Marino. Awards: 2 MID To UK June 1944.

2857 **LAA** – From UK July 1943 – (*Husky*) – Sicily – Augusta – Lentini East – Scordia – Messina. Italy – Palmi – Crotone – Bari – Foggia – Amendola – Cutella – San Vito Marino – Foggia – Naples – Capodichino. Awards: 2 MID. November 1944 Disbanded.

2858 **LAA** – From UK July 1943 – (*Husky*) – Sicily – Augusta – Lentini West – Pelagonia – Milazzo East – Messina. Italy – Reggio – Bari – Foggia – Madna – Campomarino – Foggia – Naples. To UK June 1944.

2859 **LAA** – From UK July 1943 – (*Husky*) – Sicily – Agnone – Lentini East – San Francesco – Lago. To UK June 1944.

2860 **LAA** – Formed May 1943 La Marsa. Hammamet – Sousse – Bizerta. To Italy September 1943 – Salerno – Naples – Cerignola. Awards: 1MC, 1MM, 1 MID. To UK May 1944.

2861 **LAA** – Formed May 1943 La Marsa. Hammamet – Sousse – Bizerta. To Corsica February 1944 – Ajaccio – Ile Rousse. Italy – Regina – San Servero – Acerra. Awards: 1 MID. November 1944 Disbanded.

2862 **LAA** – Formed June 1943 La Marsa. Sousse – Malta – Gozo. To Sicily August 1943 – Augusta – Agnone. Italy – Grottaglie – Bari – Termoli – Cutella – Sangro – Triono. Awards: 2 MID. To UK July 1944.

2863 **LAA** – Formed June 1943 Gharmart. From 4092/4339/4346 AA Flights. La Sebala – La Marsa – Bizerta. To Italy June 1943 – Naples – Caserta. Awards: 1 MID. To UK May 1944.

2864 **LAA** – Formed June 1943 Grombalia. Lampedusa – Sousse. To Sicily June 1943 – Palermo – Syracuse – Catania. Italy – Bari – Taranto – Cap San Vito – Pozzouli. September 1944 as Rifle – Foggia – Iesi – Osimo – Santarcangelo – Foccia – Lecce. Awards: 2 MID.   To Palestine April 1945.

2865 **LAA** – Formed June 1943 Bone. To Sicily October 1943 – Catania. Italy – Taranto – Grottaglie. To UK June 1944.

2866 **LAA** – Formed June 1943 Setif – Bone – Tingley. To Corsica December 1943 – Ajaccio. Italy – Bastia – Pianosa Island – Sisco – Leghorn – Fano – Rimini – Ravenna – Fertcara.. Austria – Klagenfurt. Italy – Codroito. Awards: 1 MID. April 1946 Disbanded.

2867 **LAA** – Formed June 1943 Phillipeville. Protville – Bizerta. To Italy October 1943 – Salerno – Naples – Ponza – Foggia. Yugoslavia – Vis – Italy – Pomigliano – Bagnoli – Miseno –

Bacoli. Awards: 2 US Soldier's Medals, 1 MID. November 1944 Disbanded.

2868 **LAA** – Formed June 1943 Protville. Hammam Lif – Bizerta. To Sicily September 1943 – Palermo – Naples. To UK June 1944.

2869 **LAA** – Formed June 1943 La Sebala. Cap Serrat – La Sebala – Bizerta. To Sardinia November 1943 – Cagliari – Sassari – Naples. To UK June 1944.

2870 **LAA** – Formed June 1943 Maison Blanche. Setif. Awards: 2 MID. January 1944 Disbanded.

2900 **LAA** – From Middle East Command May 1944. Brindisi – Campomarino – Pescara – San Servero – Acerra.    November 1944 Disbanded.

2902 **LAA** – From Middle East Command August 1944. Taranto – Barese. Greece – Kalamaki – Pireaus – Hassani – Crete. February 1945 to Egypt.

2904 **LAA** – From Middle East Command July 1943.  Sicily (*Husky*) – Syracuse – Lentini West – Catania. To Italy – Reggio –
Bari – Foggia – Termoli – Canne – Campomarino – Vasto. Febrary 1944 Disbanded.

2905 **LAA** – From Middle East Command November 1943. Tunis – Italy – Naples – Tortorella – Cerignola – Naples. To UK November 1944.

2906 **LAA** – From Middle East Command July 1943. Sicily (*Husky*) – Syracuse – Lentini East – Catania. Italy – Reggio – Salerno – Naples – Capodichino – Foggia. January 1944 Disbanded.

2907 **LAA** – From Middle East Command June 1944. Italy – Taranto – Foggia – Steraparone – Acerra. November 1944 Disbanded.

2908 **Field** – From Middle East Command August 1944. Italy – Taranto – Bari – Altamura. Greece – Katakolon – Patras – Athens – Glifada – Hassani – Crete – Athens. Awards: 2 MM, 18 MID. March 1946 to Palestine.

2913 **LAA** – From Middle East Command July 1944. Italy – Taranto – Cutella – San Vito – Fermo – Falconara – Naples. November 1944 Disbanded.

2914 **LAA** – From Middle East Command July 1944. Italy – Taranto – Foggia – San Servero – Biferno – Bari. Yugoslavia – Prykos. Austria – Udine – Moderndorf – Graz. March 1946 Disbanded.

2915 **LAA** – From Middle East Command May 1944. Italy – Taranto – Cutella – Sinello – Loreto – Iese – Naples. November 1944 Disbanded.

**2923** **LAA** – From Middle East Command July 1944. Italy – Altamura – Canne. Greece: Araxos – Piraeus – Kalamaki – Glifada – Klim – Kifissia. Italy – Acerra as Rifle – San Spirito. Awards: 1 MID March 1945 to Palestine.

**2924** **Field** – From Middle East Command August 1944. Italy – Taranto – San Spirito – Altamura. Greece – Athens – Kalamaki – Salonika – Sedes. March 1945 to Palestine.

**2925** **LAA** – From Middle East Command July 1943. Sicily (*Husky*) – Pachino – Lentini East – Catania. Italy – Grottaglie – Gioia del Colle – Foggia. Awards: 4 MID. November 1943 Disbanded.

**2926** **LAA** – June 1944 from Middle East Command. Italy – Taranto – Altamura – Biferno. Greece – Piraeus – Hassani – Elleniko – Araxos – Kifissia – Patras – Austria – Klagenfurt – Graz. March 1946 Disbanded.

**2932** **LAA** – From Middle East Command July 1944. Italy – Taranto – Foggia – Regina – Termoli – Canne – Bari. Yugoslavia – Vis. Italy – Ancona – Ravenna. Austria – Udine – Klagenfurt – Moderndorf – Graz. March 1946 Disbanded.

**2933** **LAA** – From Middle East Command July 1944. Italy – Taranto – Tortorella – Foggia – Naples. November 1944 Disbanded.

**2934** **LAA** – From Middle East Command May 1943. Malta – Luqa – Hal Far – Ta'kali. Awards: 1 MID. January 1944 to UK.

**2969** **Rifle** – Formed Acerra March 1945. To Palestine April 1945. April 1946 Disbanded.

CHAPTER SEVEN

# NORTH-WEST EUROPE 1944-45

In March 1944 the RAF Regiment component in the Second Tactical Air Force was established as thirty-eight squadrons in nineteen wings, each of one LAA and one field squadron. Within a few weeks this plan was revised in three major areas: firstly, the number of LAA squadrons was increased from nineteen to twenty-five by reducing the number of field squadrons from nineteen to thirteen. Secondly, the unit establishments were changed so as to produce six armoured car squadrons and seven rifle squadrons from the personnel of the thirteen remaining field squadrons. Thirdly, the wing headquarters were restructured to enable them to exercise command of two or more squadrons of any type, depending on the tactical situation, rather than by having specific squadrons permanently allotted to them. The removal of the armoured car flights from the former field squadrons produced independent armoured car squadrons, each of twenty-four Humber 4x4 armoured reconnaissance vehicles, which added a powerful and flexible resource of speed, mobility and protection to the Regiment's capabilities in the forthcoming campaign.

The expeditionary Air Force was organized into a Command Headquarters and four operational Groups, numbered 2, 83, 84 and 85, to which the Regiment wings and squadrons were assigned in accordance with the tasking of tactical aircraft by HQ 2TAF. At the beginning of the invasion, fourteen wing headquarters and most of the LAA squadrons, with some rifle and armoured car squadrons, were placed in 83 and 84 Groups while five wing headquarters and the remaining rifle and armoured car squadrons were shared by 2 and 85 Groups.

The part which the RAF Regiment played in the invasion of France in June 1944 (Operation *Overlord*), the liberation of much of North-West Europe and the final German surrender in May 1945 can be divided into five operational phases. The first of these was the landing on the Normandy beaches in June 1944, the occupation and defence of airfields in the beachhead, the build-up in July and preparations for the battle of France which began in August.

The second phase followed the land battles which enabled the American, British and Canadian armies to break through the German defences and strike out into France. The Regiment squadrons in 2 and 85 Groups were largely engaged in supporting the air intelligence and reconnaissance teams which entered Luftwaffe airfields and installations, including control centres, radar stations and weapon stores, while the land battle was still in progress. In 83 and 84 Groups the Regiment wings and squadrons were employed in occupying, clearing and defending the captured airfields from which tactical aircraft operated in supporting the British and Canadian armies' thrusts from Normandy towards Belgium and Holland. To assist in maintaining the momentum of the air effort, Regiment squadrons assisted in ferrying aviation fuel to forward airstrips and refuelling and rearming fighter aircraft between sorties while continuing to provide LAA and ground defence for the airfields from which the aircraft were operating.

The third phase followed in September and October 1944 when, as well as occupying and defending airfields in the Low Countries, Regiment wings consisting of rifle and armoured car squadrons were called upon to reinforce infantry and armoured units of the British and Canadian armies which were overstretched in holding the line of the River Maas and the Wilhelmina and Leopold Canals on the flank of 21st Army Group's main line of advance. November and December saw the concentration of Regiment units in preparation for the final assault on German territory, as well as the reaction to the Wehrmacht's unexpected attack in the Ardennes, when Regiment rifle and armoured car squadrons covered the withdrawal of sensitive RAF radar units to safety.

The fourth phase in the Regiment's contribution to victory in Europe began on New Year's Day 1945 when twenty-one squadrons based on eleven airfields in Belgium and Holland engaged some of the 800 German aircraft involved in Operation *Bodenplatte* ("Baseplate") which was designed to destroy Allied aircraft on the ground on up to twenty airfields in the Low Countries and northern France. In the ensuing months Regiment squadrons moved forward into Germany, escorting Air Technical Intelligence teams as well as securing airfields for RAF aircraft.

The final phase occurred shortly before the war ended when a number of Regiment task forces moved through the Army's forward positions into Schleswig-Holstein to occupy airfields and air force installations, and to take the surrender of some 50,000 German army, navy and air force officers and men. Other squadrons were deployed to Denmark and two Regiment wings which had been trained in mountain warfare in Scotland moved to Norway with British and Norwegian army units and secured the airfields around Oslo, Stavanger, Bergen and Tromso. In occupied Germany, the clearing of airfields and support for the teams disarming the Luftwaffe became the Regiment's final tasks.

On D-Day (6 June 1944) Colonel Rupert Preston, late of the Coldstream Guards and the senior RAF Regiment staff officer in 83 Group, arrived off the coast of Normandy in company with 1304 and 1305 Wing HQs and 2809, 2819 and 2834 LAA Squadrons. Because of congestion on the beaches, the Regiment force could not get ashore until the following day (D+1) when they landed on Juno Beach, where they were joined by 2817 and 2876 LAA Squadrons whose crossing from Gosport had been disrupted by an attack by German E-boats during the night. LCT46, which was carrying 2817 Squadron, was hit by shells from a German coastal battery and several members of the squadron were killed or badly wounded. LCT43, with 2876 Squadron on board came alongside and took off the living and the dead before LCT46 began to sink.

Flight Lieutenant Philip Silk of 2817 Squadron did not have a prayer book to hand but he used his Bible to conduct an improvised funeral service by reading from 2 Corinthians as the dead were buried at sea. After a very wet landing, which involved wading ashore in five feet of water, Silk and his flight carried out a reconnaissance, but found his squadron's objective, Le Fresne Camilly, still in German hands. After a night spent in the open in the reassuring company of a squadron of British tanks, Silk was able to link up with the remainder of his unit and to locate the squadron's vehicles and guns among the mass of equipment in the beachhead. By D+3 2817 Squadron was deployed on the airfield at Grange-sur-Mer, where the squadron found it necessary to send out fighting patrols to clear the surrounding woods of German snipers.

From then until mid-August the narrow foothold on the coast of France was filled by a constant stream of Army and Air force units, among which were nineteen Regiment wing HQs and thirty squadrons, of which eighteen were LAA squadrons. The latter were all deployed, and regularly in action against enemy aircraft, at the airfields and landing grounds from which RAF aircraft were operating. Near the coast, these were at Grange-sur-Mer, St Croix-sur-Mer, Courselles-sur-Mer, Graye-sur-Mer and Beny-sur-Mer; further inland were St Andre, Martragny, Ellon, Bazenville, Carpiquet, Cristot and Plumetot. 2834 LAA Squadron, whose landing had been delayed from D+1 to D+2, was deployed at Bazenville by 2330 hrs on D+2 and thus became the first Regiment squadron to be in action in France. With 359 LAA Battery of the Royal Artillery, also at Bazenville, both were constantly engaging enemy aircraft and, when the air situation permitted, the Regiment gunners assisted the hard-pressed ground crews to turn the fighter aircraft round by refuelling and rearming them in between sorties. At Cristot, later in the month, 2819 Squadron achieved a measure of immortality when the war artist Frank Wootton painted

Corporal Turner and ACs Reynolds, Swabey and Jones manning their Bofors gun on a warm summer's day in Normandy. The original of that painting now hangs in the RAF Museum at Hendon.

Although the LAA squadrons had been the first Regiment units to land in Normandy in order to provide defence against enemy aircraft, the situation on the airfields was complicated by 88mm and 210mm artillery which shelled some of the airstrips at long range, as well as by small arms fire from small parties of German infantrymen who were still concealed among the wooded features which overlooked the airfields. Derrick Dean, who served in 2876 Squadron, recalled that personnel of his squadron had to be withdrawn from their anti-aircraft guns at St Croix-sur-Mer and formed into fighting patrols to drive out the enemy troops who were harassing operations on the airfield from the direction of the village of Creully.

The Allied breakout began in August and the British Army struck south to capture Caen (where one of the defending enemy formations was the 16th Luftwaffe Division) and then west via the Falaise Gap to the Seine, Rouen, Beauvais , Brussels and Antwerp. The aircraft of 83 and 84 Groups moved forward to keep close to the Army formations which they were supporting and, once the Regiment's armoured car and rifle squadrons had cleared captured airfields, the LAA squadrons deployed to defend them against enemy air attack. At the same time the Regiment squadrons in 2 and 85 Groups were tasked to escort RAF Air Technical Intelligence (ATI) teams as they probed forward in order to reach secret German installations before they could be destroyed by the retreating enemy forces. In August 1315 Wing, with 2717 Rifle and 2757 Armoured Car Squadrons, and an ATI team were the first RAF units to enter Rouen. 2729 Rifle Squadron took an ATI team into Bayeux, and was the first British unit to reach Trouville. Detachments from 2806 Armoured Car and 2726 Rifle Squadrons escorted ATI teams to the German radar sites at Mont Pincon and Houlgate, where they attracted heavy artillery and mortar fire from German positions. Flights from 2806 Armoured Car and 2827 Rifle Squadrons escorted another ATI team to the flying bomb installations in the quarries at Hautmesnils, which were also under enemy fire. 2798 Armoured Car Squadron, which had landed on Omaha Beach under American command shortly after D-Day, advanced with General Patton's 3rd US Army from Rennes and was tasked with selecting and securing a radar site on Longchamps racecourse in the Bois de Boulogne. Entering Paris with the leading American and French troops on 25 August, 2798 Squadron became the first British unit to enter the city.

2897 had been deployed on Operation *Diver* in the South-East of England when it was selected to become a special duties unit in July 1944. Withdrawn for re-equipment and training as a rifle squadron, two flights were flown to France to become the personal protection force for the AOC-in-C 2TAF, Sir Trafford Leigh-Mallory, and when Supreme Headquarters Allied Expeditionary Forces (SHAEF) was established at Versailles in September the remainder of 2897 Squadron crossed the Channel to Utah Beach and joined the advance party to form the dedicated RAF Regiment guard force at SHAEF for the remainder of the war.

Meanwhile, the Regiment wings and squadrons in 83 and 84 Groups advanced on an axis north of Paris towards Brussels and Antwerp, occupying and defending airfields, clearing mines and booby traps, ferrying aviation fuel to forward airstrips and assisting in the refuelling and rearming of tactical aircraft. As the German army withdrew from northern France, garrisons were left in the Channel ports in order to deny their use to British forces for as long as possible. Although Le Havre, Boulogne and Calais were taken by British and Canadian forces by October, Dunkirk had not been captured by the time that 21st Army Group was heavily engaged in Holland and Belgium, and in order to maintain the siege 2831, 2856, 2862 and 2863 Rifle Squadrons were detached, on rotation, to reinforce the Polish and Czech brigades which finally captured Dunkirk in early 1945.

2871 Armoured Car Squadron was with the leading elements of the Army which liberated Brussels on 3 September before going on to Eindhoven where it seized the Philips factory complex and secured the nearby airfield. The German defence line on the Albert Canal from Antwerp to Maastricht extended for sixty miles and was thinly held by the Luftwaffe troops of the German 1st Parachute Army, consisting of eight German Air Force parachute regiments, supplemented by air and ground crews who had no aircraft to fly or maintain. It is therefore possible that the ground troops of the opposing air forces may have encountered each other as the RAF Regiment dashed forward to occupy the Dutch airfields at Eindhoven, Volkel and Grave.

The American and British airborne assaults on Nijmegen and Arnhem, which were in progress at the time, left only a narrow British-held salient south of Nijmegen while the Germans held the line of the Wilhelmina Canal. Although 2781 Armoured Car and 2726 Rifle Squadrons were deployed to screen the approaches to the airfield at Eindhoven, they were not in sufficient strength to provide adequate defence against a determined attack. Reinforcements in the form of 1301 Wing, with 2781 Armoured Car Squadron and 2729 and 2827

Rifle Squadrons under command, arrived without delay and were soon joined by 1302 Wing with three LAA squadrons, 2703, 2817 and 2876, whose gunners went into the line as riflemen along the canal from Tilburg to Eindhoven. In common with other squadrons, 2827 had to hold a wide front along the canal opposite a German battalion and tried to give the impression of being more than just an infantry company equivalent by carrying out aggressive patrolling across the canal and using its medium mortars to engage the enemy whenever movement was seen. The weight of fire was increased by the attachment of 2729 Squadron's mortar flight, and these tactics were successful in deterring the enemy from crossing the canal. In December 1944, by entering the village of Birgden to relieve the support company of the 4th Wiltshires, 2827 Rifle Squadron became the first RAF Regiment unit to set foot on German soil.

Rifle and armoured car squadrons were again detached to Army command in response to appeals for reinforcements to hold the line of the River Maas and the Leopold Canal. 1313 Wing, with 2757 Armoured Car and 2816 Rifle Squadrons, was assigned to the Canadian Army and deployed in the Moerkerke-Damme sector to carry out patrolling and medium mortar fire support tasks along the river line. Directed by Flight Sergeant Albert Greening from a variety of observation posts, including one in a church tower, which attracted unwelcome attention from the enemy, 2816 Squadron's mortar flight fired over 2,000 high explosive and smoke bombs at enemy positions in two weeks of intensive operation. Greening was subsequently awarded the Military Medal in recognition of his constant exposure to enemy fire while controlling his squadron's 3″ mortars. Elsewhere, during the sometimes confused fighting in this area, an anti-tank troop of the Royal Artillery was cut off and surrounded by the enemy. Flying Officer Norman Page's rifle flight of 2816 Squadron was ordered to rescue the trapped British sub-unit, an action for which Page was awarded the Military Cross.

Lieutenant-Colonel Kaye's 1315 Wing, with 2717 and 2719 Rifle and 2777 Armoured Car Squadrons, replaced 1313 Wing in the Moerkerke-Damme sector. Here Kaye conducted a masterly defence, integrating his squadrons with the Manitoba Dragoons and other Canadian units holding the river line. Flying Officers George Talbot and Dudley Hunt, Sergeant Eric Rodgers and Corporal Ronald Simpson, of 2717 Rifle Squadron, and Flight Lieutenants John Higginson and John Budd and LAC John Wilkinson of 2777 Armoured Car Squadron all received commendations for gallantry during those operations.

1313 Wing was then redeployed in the Canadian sector, with 2713 and 2798 Rifle and 2809 and 2742 Armoured Car Squadrons under command. While the mortar flight of 2798 Squadron was supporting an

attack by 43rd Divisional Reconnaissance Regiment at Wamel LAC
Thomas Davies saved the lives of a mortar detachment by dealing with
a misfired mortar bomb before it could explode, an act of bravery for
which he was awarded the Military Medal.

2724 Rifle Squadron had landed at Ostend from Tilbury in November
and by December was in the Canadian sector, holding a sector of the
canal at Capelle-Warpic. A successful patrol across the canal, in which
three enemy soldiers were killed and another taken prisoner, provoked a
tit-for-tat response. The next night a German patrol broke into the
squadron HQ building and a fierce hand-to-hand fight took place before
the enemy were driven out and back across the canal.

In the British sector 2827 Rifle and 2781 Armoured Car Squadrons
were operating under command of 1st Oxford & Bucks Light Infantry
when Flying Officer John Wild of 2781 Squadron won a Military Cross.
An excellent marksman, he had volunteered for a series of sniping tasks
as well as commanding observation posts on the banks of the Wilhelmina
Canal and it was on one of the latter occasions that his position was
attacked by a strong enemy patrol. Using grenades and his pistol, Wild
killed the enemy commander and wounded others, causing the survivors
to withdraw rapidly to the safety of German positions on the opposite
bank. Also in the British sector at that time, and attached to the Guards
Armoured Division, 2726 Rifle Squadron was placed under command of
2nd Irish Guards to hold part of the River Maas defence line.

The clutch of airfields in Holland, south of the River Maas between
Eindhoven and Nijmegen (Heesch, Volkel, Helmond and Gilze Rijen)
was of considerable importance to the RAF in supporting the 21st Army
Group's drive into Germany. Given the virtual elimination of the

*Corporal Wilkins, LAC Clay and LAC Freed manning a captured German Spandau LMG
on an airfield in Holland in 1944.* (IWM-CL.1397)

*40mm Bofors Detachment B.11 of 2875 LAA Squadron shooting down an attacking Me262A-2a Sturmvogel of III/KG51 based at Hopsten/Rheine near Osnabruck. This action took place at the RAF forward airfield of Helmond, near Eindhoven, on 26th November 1944 and was the first occasion on which a jet aircraft was destroyed by ground fire.* (From an original painting by Phil May)

Luftwaffe from the skies, it was both irritating and inconvenient to discover that the Germans could operate their new jet fighter/ bomber, the Me262, with impunity, as its performance outclassed the RAF's conventional piston-engined fighters. However, on 26 November 1944 an overconfident Me262 pilot attacked Helmond once too often, and was promptly shot down by 2875 LAA Squadron's B.11 gun detachment. This was the first occasion on which a jet aircraft had been destroyed by ground fire, but it was by no means the last. On 17 and 18 December a total of eighteen Me262s attacked the airfield at intervals during the day and the guns of 2873 and 2875 Squadrons damaged several of the attackers, causing at least two of them to crash within a few miles of the airfield. In February 1945 Sergeant Pollard's B.6 gun detachment of 2809 LAA Squadron shot down another Me262 over the airfield at Volkel. The final appearance of Me262s over Volkel was in April 1945, when yet another fell to 2809 Squadron's guns.

Forced to consider other ways of attacking airfields, the Germans resorted to using V1 flying bombs, whose launch sites were now too far from England to be able to continue attacking London, against area targets in Europe. Antwerp had been on the German V1 target list since its liberation by the Allies and, as the RAF moved closer to the V1 launch sites, airfields came under increasingly heavy flying bomb attacks. At Volkel a V1 set an ammunition truck belonging to 2874 LAA Squadron on fire; there was considerable collateral damage to buildings and other vehicles but the exploding 40mm ammunition threatened to spread the damage to aircraft on the airfield. 2874 Squadron personnel, led by the SWO, Warrant Officer Patrick Maguire, risked their lives in bringing the situation under control before more damage could be caused. WO Maguire was awarded the MBE and Sergeant Harry Brown the BEM for their leadership and gallantry in carrying out this operation. Elsewhere, casualties and damage were frequently caused by flying bombs, for which no organized defence of the pattern established in SE England, existed. Apart from the effects of V1 attacks on RAF airfields, personnel on leave in local towns found themselves at risk; a flying bomb which hit a cinema in Antwerp killed twenty-six RAF personnel, including four airmen of 2757 Armoured Car Squadron.

In December 1944 the Wehrmacht launched its last desperate gamble to disrupt the Allied advance by striking at the junction between the American and British armies in France. Twenty German divisions from the 5th and 6th Panzer Armies erupted from the wooded hills of the Ardennes and struck at the five American divisions which stood between them, the River Meuse, Antwerp and the rear echelons of the British and Canadian armies in Belgium and Holland. Although RAF airfields were not threatened by the initial impetus of these attacks, the RAF's 72 Wing, with its forward radars and wireless interception units, certainly was. 2811 Rifle with 2770 and 2804 Armoured Car Squadrons formed 72 Wing's covering force which enabled the technical units and their Regiment squadrons to fight their way through the confused situation which developed to the west of Bastogne as German special

*Wreckage of the Me262-2a shot down by 2875 Squadron at Helmond on 26 November 1944.* (Crown Copyright/MOD)

forces in American vehicles and uniforms spread alarm and despondency in what had been the rear area. German parachutists established roadblocks in an attempt to delay retreating units until the advancing panzer formations could reach them, but the Regiment squadrons forced their way through those they encountered. Eventually all the vital equipment was withdrawn to safety in its cumbersome vehicles and trailers, despite the inclement weather and the poor roads and tracks which had to be used, and the morale of the personnel of 6080 Signals Unit was raised considerably when they learned that the Regiment had rescued the safe with their pay in it as well!

On 31 December 1944 the RAF Regiment force level in 2TAF was seventeen wing HQs, 19 LAA squadrons, twenty rifle squadrons and 6 armoured car squadrons, a total of forty-five squadrons and an increase of almost 20% on the original D-Day planning figure.

On New Year's Day 1945 it was the Luftwaffe's turn to stake everything on a final throw of the dice: Operation *Bodenplatte*. By scraping together almost every serviceable fighter aircraft in the West, a force of almost 800 Me109s, FW190s and Me262s launched unexpected low level attacks on some twenty Allied airfields in northern

*LAC Bassett in the turret of a 2777 Squadron armoured car overlooking a Typhoon wing dispersal in Holland in 1944.* (IWM-CL.2103)

France, Holland and Belgium between 0900 and 1030hrs that morning. About half the attacking force was directed against the eleven RAF airfields in that area and although the RAF lost over one hundred aircraft on the ground, which were soon replaced, the Luftwaffe lost over twice that number in the air, and those could never be replaced.

The close liaison which the Regiment staff officers at the various group headquarters maintained with their Regiment units was exemplified at Eindhoven where Colonel Rupert Preston was paying a routine visit to 1304 Wing and its three LAA squadrons when the first wave of German aircraft, led by the Me262 jets, strafed the airfield. When the attack began Colonel Preston was standing by a 40mm gun position and, conscious of the fact that he was the senior RAF Regiment officer present, lost no time in directing the LAA fire at the numerous targets over the airfield. During the attacks the three LAA Squadrons (2703, 2773 & 2817) fired 2,750 40mm rounds at seventy attacking aircraft and destroyed at least six for the loss of two airmen killed and seven wounded. In the heat of the action a clip of 40mm ammunition jammed in the feed mechanism of one of 2773 Squadron's Bofors guns and, in accordance with gun drill procedures, the loader released the firing pedal and called out "Stoppage held" to inform the other members of the gun detachment that firing had stopped because of a mechanical fault. One of the two gunlayers, still tracking the target through his sights, shouted back "**** the stoppage, keep firing". Without the opportunity to change overheated gun barrels during the lengthy period of the attack, many of the 40mm barrels were glowing a dull cherry-red by the time firing ceased. 2806 Armoured Car Squadron was also on the airfield and added to the hail of fire over the airfield by firing its vehicle-mounted machine guns at every enemy aircraft which came within range.

At Ophoven the fifty attacking aircraft were engaged by 2794 and 2876 LAA Squadrons which fired 705 40mm rounds between them and claimed twenty-three hits, destroying six enemy aircraft and damaging nine others. Corporal Hugh Adair of 2876 Squadron was awarded the Military Medal for keeping his gun in action despite a series of direct attacks on his position by enemy aircraft.

At Volkel the three LAA squadrons ((2784, 2809 & 2834) were unable to open fire at the first wave of attacking aircraft as RAF aircraft were taking off at the same time. Once the friendly aircraft were airborne, the LAA squadrons began to engage the twenty enemy aircraft attacking the airfield and destroyed five, and damaged four more, for the expenditure of 188 rounds.

Helmond was defended by 2873, 2875 and 2881 LAA Squadrons when it was attacked by thirty German aircraft. In expending a total of

114

1,937 rounds the squadrons destroyed seven enemy aircraft and damaged at least four more.

At Heesch seven enemy aircraft were destroyed, and two damaged, by the 344 rounds fired by 2734 and 2819 LAA Squadrons. Near Antwerp, the airfield at Deurne was defended by 2880 LAA Squadron and a flight of 2816 Rifle Squadron which formed part of Wing Commander (later Group Captain) Stan Cooper's 1317 Wing. Of the sixteen attacking aircraft, one was destroyed for the expenditure of 120 40mm rounds and some SAA from the rifle flight's light machine guns. In this case, enemy activity included several V1 flying bombs and this form of attack continued for several days after *Bodenplatte*.

The airfield at Evere, outside Brussels, was defended by 2800 LAA Squadron and 2742 Armoured Car Squadron. There 350 rounds of 40mm fire, supported by machine gun fire from the armoured cars, claimed three enemy aircraft destroyed and a further eight damaged.

An attack on Woensdrechte by eight Me109s and FW190s enabled 2872 LAA squadron to destroy two aircraft, and damage another, for the expenditure of only forty-four rounds of 40mm, assisted, of course, by machine gun fire from the flight of 2816 Rifle Squadron which was also at the airfield.

In terms of the disparity between defenders and attackers, the battle at the semi-deserted airfield at Grimbergen was noteworthy. Although there were no aircraft normally based there, 2777 Armoured Car Squadron and a flight of 2719 Rifle Squadron were temporarily staging at the airfield, pending a redeployment elsewhere. When twenty-four enemy aircraft appeared overhead, the only available anti-aircraft weapons available were the two squadrons' .303″ machine guns, which rapidly shot down three FW190s and damaged two others. The pilots of the three aircraft which crashed parachuted to safety and were immediately taken prisoner by the Regiment. This was some recompense for the fact that the 2719 flight commander, Flight Lieutenant Dyson, and his driver, LAC Crouch, had both been severely wounded when their jeep was strafed by a FW190.

Melsbroek was defended by the Regiment's senior squadron, 2701 LAA, with support from flights of 2717 and 2871 Rifle Squadrons. However, on 20 December reports of a possible attack on the airfield by German panzers resulted in all twelve guns being deployed in anti-tank positions and provisioned with armour-piercing ammunition. On 30 December the threat had been amended to an infantry attack and six of the LAA guns were taken out of action and their personnel deployed as infantry reinforcements for the rifle flights. Thus on the morning of 1 January only six guns, one of which was out of action for routine servicing, could be used in the LAA role when twenty-five German aircraft began their attacks on the airfield. To add to the problems facing the LAA defences, most of the ammunition at each gun position was armour-piercing solid shot, with a lesser proportion of high explosive shells. Notwithstanding this, the five guns fired a judicious mix of 300 AP and HE rounds which, assisted by the LMG fire of the rifle flights of 2717 and 2971 Squadrons, succeeded in destroying four enemy aircraft and damaging another four. Sergeant George Toye was the first detachment commander to bring his Bofors gun into action and his skill and courage in continuing to engage the enemy, despite sustained strafing by enemy aircraft which caused casualties among his detachment, was recognized by the award of the Military Medal.

Thus, for the expenditure of just over 7,500 rounds of 40mm ammunition, and about 5,000 rounds of .303″ ammunition, forty-six of the 335 German aircraft which attacked the eleven RAF airfields were destroyed, and a further forty-two were damaged by the RAF Regiment alone. This undoubtedly enhanced the overall awareness of the important contribution which the Regiment was making to tactical air operations and by mid-February there were sixty-eight RAF Regiment squadrons, thirty-one rifle, twenty-eight LAA and six armoured car, in 2TAF; an increase of 51% in the force level over a period of six weeks.

2805 Rifle squadron had landed at Tilques from Dover in January 1945 and in April it was ordered to force a crossing of the Ems-Weser Canal to open a route towards airfields in Germany. Although the end of the war was only a few weeks away, the Germans continued to fight resolutely in defence of their homeland and the action cost the lives of Flying Officer Roberts and LAC Doherty, with six NCOs and airmen wounded. Among the other reinforcing units which had landed with 2805 Squadron was 2814 Rifle Squadron which, by the end of April, had crossed the Rhine at Wesel and advanced through the bombed rubble of Hamm to reach Hamelin on the River Weser.

Also participating in these thrusts into Germany was 2781 Armoured Car Squadron which linked up with 2805 Rifle Squadron after its crossing of the Ems-Weser Canal to occupy the airfield at Achmer, between Hannover and Wunstorf. The rifle squadron moved out to the airfield perimeter and immediately came under heavy fire from enemy positions overlooking the airfield. Flying Officer John Millar, commanding "F" Troop of the armoured car squadron, took his troop to the scene and returned fire at the enemy while loading 2805 Squadron's wounded into his vehicles. Further offensive action by the armoured cars made the enemy withdraw and Millar was subsequently awarded the Military Cross for his initiative and gallantry under fire.

Achmer, however, still had a sting in its tail and, when 2831 Squadron was engaged in clearing mines from the airfield a few days later, delayed-action fuses detonated hidden charges in a nearby ammunition dump, causing casualties to Army, RAF and RAF Regiment personnel working nearby on the airfield. Prompt reaction by Corporal Whyte and LACs Northmore and Webb, of 2831 Squadron, saved the lives of injured personnel and stabilized the situation. All three were awarded the British Empire Medal in recognition of their efforts.

In April 2856 Rifle Squadron, relieved from its involvement in the siege of Dunkirk, was tasked to secure the German airfield at Fassberg, which had been carved out of extensive pine forests in the large plain between Celle and Luneburg. Although the airfield was occupied without difficulty, small parties of German troops were holding out in the nearby villages and woods and skirmishing went on for several days until the squadron was able to clear the area and hand it over to 2858 Rifle Squadron, before moving to Hamburg to join one of the task forces which began the occupation of Schleswig-Holstein at the beginning of May.

Having assisted in clearing the debris from the airfield at Eindhoven after *Bodenplatte*, 2827 Rifle Squadron resumed its normal role and in April was engaged in seizing the German village of Everson. The eighteen prisoners, including two wounded, taken in that operation brought the squadron's total of enemy soldiers captured in the month of April to 138. The squadron then joined one of the task forces which were formed for the occupation of Schleswig-Holstein and went on to Eggebek, Schleswig and Husum before the war ended.

Although fighting was still in progress in Germany, HQ 2TAF had selected the spa town of Bad Eilsen, south-east of Minden, as its post-war headquarters and was anxious to secure it before the Army could stake a claim to it. A composite task force, based on 2804 Armoured Car Squadron and 2729 and 2807 Rifle Squadrons, was assembled and having obtained permission to pass through the Army's forward positions, reached the town after dealing with enemy roadblocks on the way. The Focke-Wulf aircraft design offices were in Bad Eilsen and the chief designer, Professor Kurt Tank, was an important figure in the aviation world. He was promptly arrested and taken to HQ 2TAF by the task force, which was relieved by 2862 Rifle Squadron as the garrison force to hold the town until the advance party of HQ 2TAF arrived.

The *Land* of Schleswig-Holstein, the most northerly of the German provinces, extends a hundred and fifty kilometres from Hamburg and the Elbe to Flensburg and the Danish border. In May 1945 it contained numerous Luftwaffe airfields and installations as well as naval bases and military garrisons. HQ 21 Army Group was, at that time, more concerned with continuing its drive eastwards to meet the Red Army as far into Germany as possible and was content to seal off the Schleswig-Holstein peninsula and deal with its contents later. The RAF did not share that view and HQ 2TAF was anxious to secure and safeguard the valuable Luftwaffe equipment which was known to be there. Accordingly, 83 Group was tasked to employ its RAF Regiment wings and squadrons to occupy Schleswig-Holstein before any cease-fire was agreed with the German military authorities.

Four days before the war ended nine RAF Regiment task groups, drawn from rifle, armoured car and LAA squadrons, rolled across the start line between Hamburg and Lübeck with orders to seize all Luftwaffe assets as far as the Danish border, to disarm enemy personnel and to place general, flag and air officers under arrest. As the war was still in progress there were, inevitably, some tense confrontations between the Regiment task groups and the commanders of hardline German units, notably the SS and Kriegsmarine, who saw no reason to allow British troops through their lines until a cease-fire had been agreed. That the Regiment task force commanders succeeded in persuading some of the most extreme elements of the German military establishment to back down without a fight was due to a combination of diplomacy, tact, bluff and, as it turned out later, German uncertainty as to exactly with whom they were dealing. The subsequent interrogation of German officers and soldiers revealed that many were under the impression that, given the devastation which the RAF had inflicted on the German homeland, the RAF Regiment was the British counterpart of the Waffen SS, and therefore not to be trifled with. As an example of this, Squadron Leader Mark Hobden's task force of less than fifty officers and men was temporarily halted at the bridge at Rendsburg by an SS panzer battalion but after some forthright discussions the German colonel gave way and the small Regiment force crossed the bridge and went on to reach its objectives. When the Regiment reached Flensburg, Grand Admiral Doenitz, who was Hitler's appointed successor, was found and arrested.

After occupying sixteen major airfields and securing the aircraft and equipment on them, the various Regiment task groups took the surrender of the 50,000 German soldiers, sailors and airmen in the region and disarmed them. Over a thousand Allied prisoners of war were freed from prison camps and returned to the UK, but the major task was that of feeding, clothing and housing the large number of starving Russian prisoners who had been kept in appalling conditions in slave labour camps throughout Schleswig-Holstein.

A detachment of 2819 LAA Squadron formed the tenth Regiment task force which flew into Kastrup, in Denmark, where Luftwaffe

*Crown Prince Olaf of Norway inspects a Guard of Honour provided by 2830 Rifle Squadron (Flt Lt Lipscombe & Fg Off Dutton) at Fornebu in June 1945.* (IWM-CL.2184)

ground crews were busy marshalling RAF aircraft as they landed. Instead of enjoying the bright lights of Copenhagen as he had hoped, Corporal Eric Westrope, who had waded ashore on Juno Beach with the squadron on D+1, found himself stationed at Kastrup to deal with the flood of senior German officers who arrived there by air, intent on surrendering to the British rather than the Russians.

Several RAF Regiment squadrons had been trained in mountain warfare techniques in Scotland, where they exercised alongside Norwegian army units in preparation for the invasion of Norway. 1318 Wing HQ, with 2737, 2830 and 2949 Rifle Squadrons, embarked at Leith with elements of the 3rd and 52nd Infantry Divisions and sailed for Norway shortly after VE-Day. 2737 Squadron disembarked at Kristiansand and and occupied the airfields at Kjevic and Lister, where they took the surrender of 3,000 Luftwaffe officers and men. 2830 Squadron went on to the airfields at Tromso, Bardufoss and Fornebu while 2949 Squadron landed at Stavanger and took over the airfields at Sola and Gardemoen, where it was later relieved by 2791 Squadron from Germany. When it was discovered that the Luftwaffe presence in Norway was larger than expected, 2875 Squadron was airlifted from Flensburg to Gardemoen and was followed by 1336 Wing HQ and 2847 Squadron which were sent to Trondheim from the UK. The Regiment presence in Denmark, which was originally only 2819 Squadron at Kastrup, was also increased by redeploying 2740 and

2827 Squadrons from Germany to Vandel and Vaerlose.

In July 1945 the last Regiment units were withdrawn from Scandinavia and large-scale redeployments had already begun in occupied Germany. Some of the Regiment wings and squadrons were stationed on airfields which had been selected for long-term use by the RAF, but most of the twenty wing headquarters and seventy-eight squadrons which had served in 2TAF in 1944-45 were returned to the UK or disbanded in situ. Some were briefly retained to assist in the work of the RAF's air disarmament teams but by the end of 1946 only four wing headquarters and twelve squadrons of the RAF Regiment remained in Germany as part of the British Air Forces of Occupation.

## THE CAMPAIGN IN NORTH-WEST EUROPE IN RETROSPECT

The tactical air operations carried out by the RAF from Normandy to the Baltic were, in many ways, the classic model for the employment of the RAF Regiment in a major war. Success was ensured by the detailed planning and training which was carried out in the UK well before the invasion of France began, and by the highly effective command and staff structure which directed operations throughout the campaign. The inclusion of an RAF Regiment team, led by Wing Commander CW Mayhew, in the *Overlord* planning staff (and later, as Group Captain Mayhew at HQ SHAEF) ensured that the correct balance of Regiment forces was included in 2TAF and that the role of the RAF Regiment was clearly set out in the directives prepared for senior RAF Commanders and their staffs.

With an air commodore Regiment post, filled by Brigadier M. A. Green OBE MC late of the Northamptonshire Regiment, at HQ 2TAF, group captain posts (filled by colonels) at 83 and 84 Groups and wing commander posts (filled by lieutenant-colonels) at 85 and 2 Groups, there were no gaps between Regiment and Air Staff decisions and their implementation at unit level where the close relationship between flying units and Regiment squadrons ensured the best possible support for air operations in an hostile environment. Led by Brigadier Green, who had a distinguished record as a young infantry officer in the First World War, followed by considerable experience as a staff officer, the colonels and lieutenant-colonels who served with the Regiment HQ staffs and commanded wings brought with them a background of battle experience which stood the operational squadrons in good stead as they fought their way into Germany.

The flexible structure, which enabled squadrons of different types to be grouped under a wing headquarters as required for particular operations maximized the effectiveness of the Regiment organization by allowing squadrons to be redeployed at short notice in the knowledge that an adequate command and control structure was available wherever it was required. When the enemy air threat diminished, LAA squadrons were switched to the ground role; when the opportunity arose to keep the ground threat to airfields at a greater distance, the Regiment reinforced the Army's forward defences where they needed strengthening. In addition, wherever and whenever the Air Force required it, the Regiment carried out a multiplicity of secondary tasks in support of aircraft operations in addition to its primary roles of ground and low-level air defence.

Apart from the Home Defence role in the United Kingdom, North-West Europe absorbed a greater proportion of RAF Regiment units than all other overseas theatres combined, and the positive results were there, close at hand, for all to see. The contribution made by the Regiment's wings and squadrons to the effectiveness of air operations within the framework of the RAF's largest and most powerful tactical air force made an overriding case for the permanent retention of the RAF Regiment in the post-war Air Force.


## WING HEADQUARTERS IN NW EUROPE 1944-1946

**1300** – Normandy D+2 – St Andre – Beauvais – Vitry – Grimbergen – Deurne – Volkel February 1945 Disbanded. October 1945 Reformed. Altona – Bad Eilsen – Buckeburg. Awards: 1 MBE

**1301** – Normandy D+9 – Martragny – Ellon – Evreaux – Evere – Eindhoven – Schleswig Holstein. June 1946 Disbanded.

**1302** – Normandy D+2 – Grange-sur-Mer – La Baronnie – St Croix – Melsbroek – Eindhoven – Wilhelmina Canal. January 1945 Disbanded. October 1945 Reformed.

**1303** – Normandy D+8 – Lantheuil – Longues – Douai – Deurne – Grave – List. April 1946 Disbanded.

**1304** – Normandy D+1 – La Valette – St Croix – Carpiquet – Beauvais – Melsbroek – Eindhoven (*Bodenplatte*). January 1945 Disbanded. October 1945 Reformed. Celle. Awards: 1 OBE

**1305** – Normandy D+1 – Bazenville – Cristot – St Andre – Volkel. Awards: 1 OBE. January 1946 Disbanded.

**1306** – Normandy D+10 – Plumetot – Volkel – Heesch. February 1945 Disbanded. October 1945 Reformed – Gatow.

1307 – Normandy D+11 – Longues – Vitry. September 1944
Disbanded. Reformed October 1944. To ACSEA November 1944.
1308 – Normandy D+11. To UK October 1944. To ACSEA November 1944.
1309 – Normandy D+2 – Courselles – Graye – Beny – Grave –
Helmond. (*Bodenplatte*). February 1945 Disbanded.
1310 – Normandy August 1944. April 1946 Disbanded.
1311 – Normandy August 1944 – Beny – Deurne – Gilze Rijen
(*Bodenplatte*) – Delmenhorst. September 1946 Disbanded.
1312 – Normandy August 1944 – Plumetot – Deurne – Grimbergen
(*Bodenplatte*). January 1945 Disbanded.
1313 – Normandy August 1944 – Wilhelmina Canal – Gutersloh.
September 1946 Disbanded.
1314 – Normandy August 1944 – Sommervieu – Carpiquet – Brionne
– Courtrai – Deurne (*Bodenplatte*). December 1946 Disbanded.
1315 – Normandy August 1944 – Rouen – Damme – Maele – Capelle
– Leopold Canal – Moerkerke – Knokke – Wahn. Awards: 1 OBE
April 1946 Disbanded.
1316 – Normandy August 1944 – Grange – Carpiquet – Merville –
Maldegem – Evere (*Bodenplatte*). January 1945 Disbanded.
October 1945 Reformed – Wahn.
1317 – Normandy D+2 – Glisy – Grimbergen – Deurne (*Bodenplatte*)
– Gatow. July 1946 Disbanded.
1318 – Normandy D+2 – St Croix – Deurne. October 1944 to UK.
To Norway May 1945. Oslo – Forus – Kjeller – Gardemoen –
Bardufoss – Tromso. July 1945 Disbanded.
1336 – Trondheim May 1945. July 1945 Disbanded. Awards: 1 Croix
de Guerre +1 MID

## SQUADRONS IN NW EUROPE 1944 – 191946

2701 **LAA** Normandy August 1944 – Melsbroek (*Bodenplatte*) –
Fassberg, Awards: 1 MM+5MID. September 1945 Disbanded.
2703 **LAA** Normandy D+8 – Eindhoven (*Bodenplatte*) – Achmer –
Celle – Flensburg. December 1945 Disbanded.
2710 **Rifle** NW Europe May 1945 – Flensburg. May 1946 Disbanded.
2713 **Rifle** Normandy August 1944 – Rennes – Caen – Brussels –
Leopold Canal – Ghent – Bonn – Luneburg.
2715 **LAA** NW Europe February 1945 – Gilze Rijen – Knokke.
December 1945 Disbanded.
2717 **Rifle** Normandy August 1944 – Rouen – Brussels – Maele –
Damme – Leopold Canal – Antwerp – Melsbroek (*Bodenplatte*) –
Celle. Awards: 4 Croix de Guerre. To Middle East October 1945.

**2719 Rifle** NW Europe November 1944 – Waspik Boven – Grimbergen (*Bodenplatte*) – Jever – Buckeburg – Detmold. May 1946 Disbanded.

**2724 Rifle** NW Europe November 1944 – Capelle – Warpik – Gilze Rijen – Fassberg – Celle – Gatow. Awards: 1 MID

**2726 Rifle** Normandy August 1944 – Eindhoven – Wilhelmina Canal – Maas – Luneburg – Lubeck – Schleswig Holstein – Vandel – Lubeck. Awards: 3 MID. March 1946 Disbanded.

**2729 Rifle** Normandy August 1944 – Bayeaux – Trouville – Wilhelmina Canal – Bad Eilsen – Gatow. 1 Order of Leopold+5 Croix de Guerre+1 MID. March 1946 Disbanded.

**2731 Rifle** NW Europe February 1945 – St Omer – Hamburg. August 1946 Disbanded.

**2734 LAA** Normandy D+11 – Beny – Brussels – Eindhoven – Volkel – Heesch (*Bodenplatte*) – Fassberg – Lubeck. Awards: 1 Croix de Guerre.December 1945 Disbanded.

**2736 LAA** Normandy D+12 – Courselle – Gilze Rijen (*Bodenplatte*) – Wunstorf. Awards: 1 MID

**2737 Rifle** Norway May 1945 – Kristianasand – Kjevic – Lister – Oslo. Awards: 4 King Haakon Medals. Dec 1945 Disbanded.

**2738 LAA** NW Europe January 1945 – St Omer – Mons – Bonn. July 1946 Disbanded.

**2740 Rifle** NW Europe February 1945 – St Omer – Weeze – Vandel – Celle – Gatow. September 1946 Disbanded.

**2741 Rifle** NW Europe January 1945 – Ghent – Liege – Detmold. August 1946 Disbanded.

**2742 Armoured Car** – NW Europe November 1944 – Maas – Waal – Evere (*Bodenplatte*) – Remagen – Bonn. Awards: 1 Order of Leopold+6 Croix de Guerre+3 MID To Middle East October 1945.

**2749 Rifle** NW Europe April 1945 – Detmold – Gutersloh – Wahn. September 1946 Disbanded.

**2750 Rifle** NW Europe December 1944 – Mons – Bonn – Achmer – Bochum – Osnabruck – Wahn. Awards: 1 Croix de Guerre

**2757 Armoured Car** – Normandy August 1944 – Rouen – Antwerp – Leopold Canal – Wunstorf – Bonn – Gütersloh – Celle. Awards: 1 Croix de Guerre+4 MID

**2760 LAA** NW Europe February 1944 – Ostend – Altona. Awards: 1 MID December 1946 Disbanded.

**2765 Rifle** NW Europe February 1945 – St Omer – Fuhlsbuttel – Schleswig Holstein – Flensburg – Sylt – Grove – Eggebek. August 1946 Disbanded.

**2768 Rifle** NW Europe February 1945 – Melsbroek – Volkel – Gilze Rijen. October 1945 Disbanded.

**2770 Rifle** NW Europe October 1944 – Strasbourg – Mutzig – Ardennes – Krefeld – Gutersloh. Awards: 1 MID

**2773 LAA** Normandy August 1944 – Eindhoven (*Bodenplatte*) – Hildesheim. Awards: 1 MID. December 1945 Disbanded.

**2777 Armoured Car** – Normandy August 1944 – Beny – Grimbergen (*Bodenplatte*) Hamburg – Fassberg – Achmer – Celle. Awards: 1 BEM+1 MID

**2781 Armoured Car** – Normandy August 1944 – Maas – Wilhelmina Canal – Hannover – Achmer – Schleswig Holstein – Sylt – Lübeck. Awards: 2 MC+3 BEM+8 MID. July 1946 Disbanded.

**2786 Rifle** NW Europe April 1945 – Ghent – Hamelin – Hamburg.

**2791 LAA** NW Europe February 1945 – Lille – Celle – Stavanger – Sola. Awards: 2 King Haakon Medals. Dec 1945 Disbanded.

**2794 LAA** Normandy D+12 – Brussels – Ophoven (*Bodenplatte*) – Schleswig Holstein – Husum – Vandel – Flensburg. December 1945 Disbanded.

**2798 Rifle** Omaha Beach D+4 – Rennes – Paris – Nijmegen – Brussels – Wamel – Waal – Walcheren – Cortenburg – Bastogne – Kiel – List – Flensburg – Wahn. Awards: 1 MM+2 Croix de Guerre+1 MID

**2800 LAA** Normandy August 1944 – Merville – Maldagem – Evere (*Bodenplatte*) – Gilze Rijen – Dedelstorf. Awards: 2 MID. December 1945 Disbanded.

**2804 Armoured Car** – Normandy September 1944 – St Croix – Ardennes – Wunstorf – Gatow. Awards: 1 MC+3 Croix de Guerre+1 MID. December 1945 Disbanded.

**2805 Rifle** NW Europe January 1945 – Ghent – Ems/Weser Canal – Osnabruck – Achmer – Luneburg – Schleswig Holstein. June 1946 Disbanded.

**2806 Armoured Car** Normandy July 1944 – Carpiquet – Beauvais – Melsbroek – Escaut – Albert Canal – Eindhoven – Luneburg – Schleswig Holstein – Sylt. Awards: 1 GM+1 Croix de Guerre+5 MID. April 1946 Disbanded.

**2807 Rifle** NW Europe February 1945 – Eindhoven – Wunstorf – Wahn. Awards: 1 Croix de Guerre+1 MID. April 1946 Disbanded.

**2809 LAA** Normandy D+1 – St Croix – Ellon – Carpiquet – Volkel (*Bodenplatte*) – Celle – Tondern – Schleswig Holstein. Awards: 1 MID. December 1945 Disbanded.

**2811 Rifle** NW Europe November 1944 – Mons – Malmedy – Laroche – Morville – Ardennes – Weikersheim – Scheede – Ghent. Awards: 1 Order of Leopold+3 Croix de Guerre. March 1946 Disbanded.

**2812 LAA** NW Europe February 1945 – Ostend – Epinoy. November 1945 Disbanded.

**2814 Rifle** NW Europe April 1945 – Antwerp – Eindhoven – Wesel – Hamm – Hamelin – Scharfoldendorf – Hildesheim. July 1946 Disbanded.

**2816 Rifle** Normandy August 1944 – St Croix – Rouen – St Pol – Moerkerke – Leopold Canal – Damme – Grimbergen – Woernsdrecht/Deurne (*Bodenplatte*) – Antwerp – Ahlhorn – Hustedt – Celle. Awards: 1 MC+1 MM+2 MID+1 Order of the Crown+1 Order of Leopold+4 Croix de Guerre. June 1946 Disbanded.

**2817 LAA** Normandy D+2 – Grange – Beauvais – Brussels – Eindhoven – Heesch (*Bodenplatte*) – Uetersen. Awards: 5 MID. December 1945 Disbanded.

**2819 LAA** Normandy D+1 – St Croix – Beny – Cristot – Brussels – Eindhoven – Heesch (*Bodenplatte*) – Luneburg – Kastrup – Schleswig – Holstein – Lübeck. Awards: 1 Croix de Guerre+2 MID. Dec 1945 Disbanded.

**2822 Rifle** NW Europe May 1945 – Copenhagen – Aarhus – Vandel – Gutersloh. April 1946 Disbanded.

**2823 Rifle** NW Europe February 1945 – Amiens – Brussels – Evere – Rheine – Fuhlsbuttel – Stade May 1946 Disbanded.

**2824 Rifle** NW Europe February 1945 – Vitry – Gilze Rijen. Awards: 1 MBE+1 MID November 1945 Disbanded.

**2826 LAA** NW Europe February 1945 – Courtrai – Lübeck – Flensburg. Awards: 1 MID December 1945 Disbanded.

**2827 Rifle** Normandy July 1944 – Cristot – St Clair – Wilhelmina Canal – Helmond – Volkel – Eindhoven – Birgden – Everson – Mettingen – Schleswig Holstein – Lübeck – Kiel – Vaerlose – Hamburg – Gütersloh. Awards:1Croix de Guerre+1MID

**2829 Rifle** NW Europe October 1944 – Gilze Rijen – Maas – Grave – Celle – Lübeck.

**2830 Rifle** Norway May 1945 – Tromso – Bardufoss – Fornebu. Awards: 1 MBE+2 MID+2 King Haakon Medals. October 1945 Disbanded.

**2831 Rifle** NW Europe October 1944 – Epinoy – Sancourt – Dunkirk – Achmer – Detmold. Awards: 3 BEM. Mar 1946 Disbanded.

**2834 LAA** Normandy D+1 – Bazenville – Carpiquet – Cristot – Boussey – St Andre – Volkel (*Bodenplatte*) – Kastrup – Flensburg. Awards: 1 MID. November 1945 Disbanded.

**2838 LAA** NW Europe February 1945 – Melsbroek – Gutersloh. December 1945 Disbanded.

**2843 Rifle** NW Europe November 1944 – Maldegem – Capelle – Gilze Rijen – Grimbergen – Delden – Scheuen – Dedelstorf – Ahlhorn.

August 1946 Disbanded.

**2844 Rifle** NW Europe May 1945 – Luneburg. March 1946 Disbanded.

**2845 Rifle** Normandy September 1944 – Lisieux – Epinoy – Vitry –
Gilze Rijen (*Bodenplatte*) – Delmenhorst. December 1945 Disbanded.

**2847 Rifle** Norway May 1945 – Trondheim – Vaernes – Lade. Awards:
1 MID. December 1945 Disbanded.

**2848 Rifle** NW Europe November 1944 – Volkel – Assche – Herford –
Magdeburg (Russian Zone) – Kladow – Gatow – Fassberg.
July 1946 Disbanded.

**2853 Rifle** NW Europe May 1945 – Traben Trabach – Bad Godesburg.
Awards: 1 MID. December 1945 Disbanded.

**2856 Rifle** NW Europe January 1945 – St Omer – Dunkirk –
Eindhoven – Damme – Diepholz – Celle – Fassberg – Schleswig
Holstein –  Husum. April 1946 Disbanded.

**2858 Rifle** NW Europe May 1945 – Maldegem – Scheuen – Wesendorf
– Fassberg – Luneburg – Celle. April 1946 Disbanded.

**2862 Rifle** NW Europe January 1945 – St Omer – Dunkirk – Rosieres
– Buckeburg – Oberkirchen – Jever – Delmenhorst.
March 1946 Disbanded.

**2863 Rifle** NW Europe November 1944 – Froyennes – Dunkirk –
Middelkirke – Gilze Rijen – Eindhoven – Wahn. Awards: 1MID.
November 1945 Disbanded.

**2865 Rifle** NW Europe January 1945 – St Omer – Mons – Mutzig –
Neustadt – Oberstein – Bad Homburg – Riefenburg – Tabarz –
Hesselburg – Bonn – Buckeburg – Bad Eilsen – Gatow.

**2868 Rifle** NW Europe April 1945 – Brussels – Rheine – Rehburg –
Wuhrden – Wunstorf – Soltau – Uetersen. Mar 1946 Disbanded.

**2871 Rifle** NW Europe October 1944 – Melsbroek (*Bodenplatte*).
December 1945 Disbanded.

**2872 LAA** Normandy August 1944 – Villon – Lille – Grimbergen –
Woernsdrecht (*Bodenplatte*) – Twente – Ahlhorn. December 1945
Disbanded.

**2873 LAA** Normandy August 1944 – Beny – Fresnoy – Fort Rouge –
St Denis – Helmond – (*Bodenplatte*) – Dedelstorf. Awards: 1 MID.
December 1945 Disbanded.

**2874 LAA** Normandy August 1944 – Martragny – Volkel (*Bodenplatte*)
– Dedelstorf. Awards: 1 MBE+1 BEM. December 1945 Disbanded.

**2875 LAA** Normandy D+12 – Les Buissons – Bazeville – Wavre –
Grave – Helmond (*Bodenplatte*) – Rheine – Celle – Fassberg –
Schleswig Holstein – Flensburg Norway: Gardemoen – Kjeller
– Lillestrom. Awards: 2 MID. + 2 King Haakon Medals.
November 1945 Disbanded.

**2876 LAA** Normandy D+2 – Coulonds – Louvain – Gossecourt – Ophoven (*Bodenplatte*) – Uetersen – Schleswig Holstein – Sylt. Awards: 1MM+1 Croix de Guerre+4 MID. June 1946 Disbanded.

**2878 Rifle** NW Europe May 1945 – Tilburg – Twente – Oldenburg – Delmenhorst. September 1946 Disbanded.

**2879 Rifle** NW Europe November 1944 – Vitry – Brussels – Eindhoven – Dortmund. May 1946 Disbanded.

**2880 LAA** Normandy August 1944 – Verdeville – Volkel – Helmond (*Bodenplatte*) – Twente – Celle – Wunstorf. June 1946 Disbanded.

**2881 LAA** Normandy August 1944 – St Croix – Verdeville – Volkel – Helmond (*Bodenplatte*) – Schleswig Holstein – Uetersen – Travemunde. November 1945 Disbanded.

**2883 Rifle** NW Europe April 1945 – Melsbroek – Suchtelen – Dankersen – Grove – Schleswig Holstein – Wahn. December 1945 Disbanded.

**2897 Rifle** Normandy August 1944 – Special Duties Squadron for AOC-in-C HQ 2TAF – Versailles – Buckeburg – Bad Eilsen.

**2949 Rifle** Norway May 1945 – Stavanger – Sola – Gardemoen – Fornebu. Awards: 5 King Haakon Medals. October 1945 Disbanded.

# CHAPTER EIGHT

# SOUTH-EAST ASIA 1942-46

The traditional military dispositions with which Great Britain normally begins its wars were nowhere more evident than in the Far East in December 1941. The pre-war plan for the defence of Singapore was based on the assumption that a Japanese attack would have to be mounted from the Japanese islands, some 3,000 miles away, and that there would be adequate warning time for reinforcements to arrive and for the invasion force to be defeated at sea. As it happened, the powerful fleet on which this plan depended was several thousand miles away, the Army's planning hinged on the Malayan jungle being impenetrable to an enemy, and the RAF lacked most of the 336 aircraft which had been deemed necessary to defend Singapore. When the attack came, the Japanese army, having advanced through China to Indo-China, was poised to strike at Singapore by crossing into Malaya without warning and without the need for a long sea voyage.

To operate effectively against enemy naval forces, the RAF's forward airfields in Malaya had been sited and constructed near the east coast in order to maximize the aircraft ranges in the area of the greatest threat, the South China Sea. The assault from nearby Indo-China presented the Army with a tactical dilemma: while the revised plan for defending Malaya against invasion required forces to be held back from the coastline, so as to counter-attack once the dispositions of the enemy were known, they could not afford to lose vital air support by leaving the RAF's forward airfields undefended. As a result, the Army was forced to adopt a tactically unsound deployment and the invading Japanese were able to outmanoeuvre the British forces and overrun four modern and well-equipped RAF bases in Malaya for their own aircraft to use in supporting the assault on Singapore, which, in its turn, fell in February 1942. Had the Army been able to conduct the land battle on its own terms by leaving airfield defence to the RAF, the campaign might well have taken a different course.

Attempts by those British personnel who had escaped from Malaya and Singapore to establish a defence line in the Dutch East Indies merely prolonged the inevitable British collapse, despite the arrival of RAF aircraft and personnel from the UK and their deployment to Palembang in Sumatra. Among these were the forerunners of the RAF

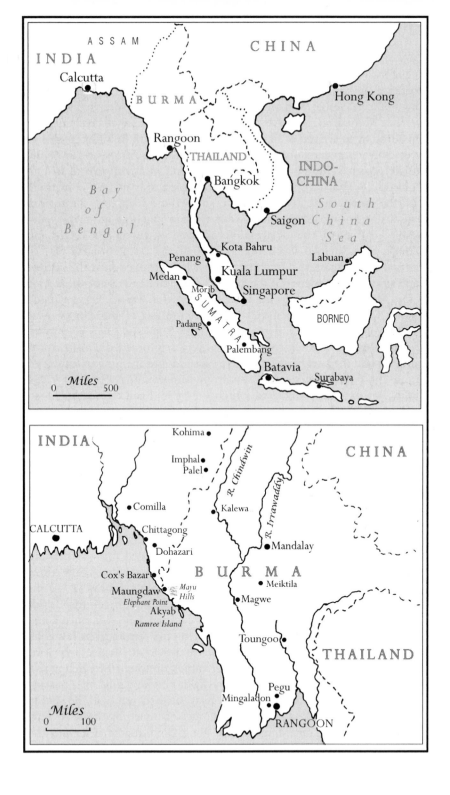

ASSAM

INDIA

Calcutta

CHINA

BURMA

Hong Kong

Rangoon

THAILAND

INDO-
CHINA

Bangkok

*Bay
of
Bengal*

Saigon

*South
China
Sea*

Kota Bahru

Penang

Kuala Lumpur

Medan

*Morib*

Singapore

*S U M A T R A*

Labuan

Padang

BORNEO

Palembang

Batavia

Surabaya

*Miles*
0        500

---

INDIA

Kohima

CHINA

Imphal
Palel

*R. Chindwin*

Comilla

Kalewa

*R. Irrawaddy*

CALCUTTA

Chittagong

Dohazari

Mandalay

Cox's Bazar

B U R M A

Maungdaw

*Mayu
Hills*

Meiktila

*Elephant Point*

Magwe

Akyab

*Ramree Island*

Toungoo

THAILAND

Pegu

Mingaladon

*Miles*
0        100

RANGOON

129

Regiment (which had only been formed in that month, and of whose existence probably no one in the Far East was aware) in the form of Pilot Officer Gough and thirty-six ground gunners, drawn from 756 Defence Squadron at RAF Eglinton and attached to 232 Fighter Squadron, who arrived at Palembang on 6 February. Reinforcements of three defence officers, one of whom was the South African-born Flying Officer Matthys Taute, and eighty-six ground gunners arrived to join them on 10 February 1942. This small group was at first concerned with the anti-aircraft defence of the airfield known as P1, the former civil airport, using Lewis and Vickers-Maxim machine guns, but were unable to prevent the destruction of twenty-two RAF aircraft and damage to a further seven on the airfield by 13 February. On 14 February 500 Japanese parachute troops were dropped near the airfield and Taute took his men into the surrounding jungle to attack the enemy before they could regroup for an assault on the airfield. With a much smaller force, Taute disrupted the concentration of more numerous enemy troops and forced them to withdraw. Such successes could not, of course, last and when the Japanese were reinforced the airfield was captured and the surviving defenders escaped into the jungle. Taute and his ground gunners made their way from Sumatra to Java in the hope of finding, or building, a boat in which they could sail to Australia, but most succumbed to malaria and the 600 or so RAF personnel in Java were soon betrayed to the Japanese by the local inhabitants. After more than three years in Japanese prison camps, Flying Officer Taute was released from captivity in September 1945 and his former commanding officer recommended him for the award of the Military Cross for his actions at Palembang in February 1942. The award was duly promulgated in 1946, making Matthys Taute the first RAF Regiment officer to win the Military Cross, and the last wartime recipient of that decoration to have the award gazetted.

The momentum of Japanese expansion continued into Burma and after the fall of Rangoon the Japanese armies advanced along three separate axes towards the Arakan, India and China. By mid-1942 the seemingly invincible Japanese army and air force had driven the British and Indian Armies, and the RAF, almost completely out of Burma and across the Indian border into Assam. During the retreat from Rangoon General Slim had flown in to the forward airfield at Magwe, which he found to be devoid of any British personnel, although Blenheims and Hurricanes were parked around the airfield. Hitching a lift in a passing truck into the town some three miles away, he discovered all the station officers and airmen relaxing in the buildings occupied by the RAF wing headquarters. The General asked the Wing Commander if he was not concerned at leaving so many aircraft completely unguarded and was told that it was not a matter which concerned the RAF as the defence of the airfield was an Army responsibility.

As it happened, at that time the local population was potentially hostile to the British, the forward units of the Japanese army were advancing and the rearguards of the retreating British Army were engaged elsewhere, so the ground threat to the airfield was considerable, but there were no soldiers to defend it. Despite the RAF's attempts to deploy AA defences to Magwe, the hastily-assembled party of ground gunners could not reach the airfield before it had been attacked by the Japanese air force and all the RAF aircraft on the ground had been destroyed and the airfield itself made unusable. Unfortunately, this was not an isolated occurrence and it was not long before the British Army in Burma was left to continue its retreat without any form of air cover. There was obviously a great deal still to be learned by all concerned.

Although there were some 4,500 RAF ground gunners in SE Asia at that time, they were, in accordance with RAF policy, spread thinly throughout RAF units. They were not organized into dedicated field or AA flights or squadrons, which could be deployed to defend the airfields where they were most needed, so their contribution to ground and air defence was minimal. There was no coherent staff structure for implementing an airfield defence policy within the command, but in October 1942 the first step was taken to reorganize what resources there were by establishing a training school, the RAF Regiment Training Centre, at Begampet, near Secunderabad, to retrain former ground gunners as members of RAF Regiment anti-aircraft flights. The first of these new units was formed in November 1942 and numbered 4351 as the beginning of a series. However, the Air Ministry in London later realized that these numbers overlapped with those which had been allocated to the AA flights in North Africa and in April 1943 the AA flights in Air Command South-East Asia (ACSEA) were ordered to be renumbered from 4401 to 4450.

The anti-aircraft flights in the Far East consisted initially of 2 officers and thirty-seven airmen equipped with eighteen .303″ Bren light machine guns, as opposed to the two officers and fifty-eight airmen, with twenty-four Browning .303″ machine guns or twelve 20mm Hispano guns, of the North African anti-aircraft flights. However, shortages of men and equipment in India delayed the completion of the programme in India and the last of the fifty AA flights which had been authorized did not become operational until the second half of 1943. A further eleven AA flights, which were raised under local arrangements in late 1943, when the supply of weapons and the availability of manpower had improved, were designated "No.1 (India) AA Flight", et seq. From 1944 onwards supplies of 20mm Hispano guns reached India and the LAA squadrons which by then had been formed from the AA flights were rearmed and reorganized, with three flights each of eight 20mm Hispanos.

Initially, the running battle between London and Delhi over RAF Regiment manpower levels had intensified after the Air Ministry's proposal to replace RAF Regiment airmen by locally-enlisted personnel was rejected by GHQ India. Reluctantly, the Air Ministry agreed to an establishment of 162 officers and 4,092 airmen of the RAF Regiment in South-East Asia, but it was not long before London revised the manning level downwards from the 141 officers and 4,549 airmen already in the Command to a figure of 2,000 all ranks. This became the subject of further argument and it was subsequently agreed that, while the future RAF Regiment establishment in ACSEA would be 152 officers and 2,358 airmen, it would not be reduced to that level until June 1944.

Group Captain J. H. Harris arrived in India in December 1942 to fill the new post of Command Defence Officer in Air Command South-East Asia and immediately began to create the proper organization and infrastructure for the formation of RAF Regiment squadrons. RAF Regiment staff posts were established at each of the seven RAF group headquarters and early in 1943 the Training Centre at Begampet was expanded to become the RAF Regiment Depot (India) with the task of forming and training field squadrons as well as continuing the production of AA flights which had been started under the aegis of the former Training Centre. The Forward Training Centre, later renamed the Forward Echelon of the RAF Regiment Depot (India), at Argatala in Assam, was opened in 1943 to provide operational training for the first six field squadrons formed in ACSEA following the completion of their basic training.

The AA flights began their operational deployments in 1943 to RAF airfields and radar installations in the Arakan and eastern Bengal, where the Japanese air force was particularly active. Chittagong, Cox's Bazar, Dohazari, Ramu, Feni, Comilla, Alipore, Dum Dum, Armada Road, Argatala and even Koggala and Ratmalana in Ceylon, were all defended by the anti-aircraft flights in 1943. At Khargpur the OC of 4412 Flight, Flight Lieutenant Macintyre-Cathles (later OC 2962 Squadron), who had clearly been trained as a draughtsman, if not as an architect, produced impeccable scale drawings for the accommodation, cookhouse, ablutions and latrines which were required for his flight, and added a detailed plan of the anti-aircraft defences of the airfield and the air loading diagrams for the move of his men, guns and equipment by

Dakota transport aircraft for good measure. Unfortunately, this model of administrative and operational planning was not adopted as a standard procedure.

Flight Lieutenant Harry Homer commanded 4438 AA Flight at Dum Dum, Santanal and Palel in 1943 and 1944, before it was disbanded and its personnel drafted to form 2967 (Field) Squadron. He compiled an entertaining story of his flight's adventures and published it after the war as *No Tigers in My Jungle*, probably the only book written about life in India and Assam from a Regiment viewpoint, although Wing Commander Randle Manwaring gave an outline of his service in the Regiment in the UK and ACSEA in his autobiography *The Good Fight*.

The first squadrons which were formed between April and July 1943 were originally numbered 2901 to 2906, until Air Ministry realized that the 2900-2935 block had already been allocated to the Middle East Air Force which was raising its own field squadrons at the same time. HQ ACSEA was thereupon ordered to renumber its first six RAF Regiment squadrons from 2941 to 2946.

The result of enemy attacks on the important airfields in the Imphal Plain saw the deployment of 4408 Flight to Imphal and 4430, 4440 and 4444 Flights to Palel in October 1943. 2941 and 2944 Field Squadrons were flown in to secure the airfield against ground attack, but, because of the terrain, the squadron positions were widely dispersed in the surrounding hills and had to be resupplied by pack mules. By early 1944 all fifty AA flights, plus eleven (India) AA flights were deployed operationally to defend airfields and radar sites in Ceylon, Bengal and Assam. Imphal and Palel in particular attracted considerable attention from the enemy once the British offensive began in March 1944 and air attacks, and shelling by Japanese artillery, caused casualties to personnel and damage to aircraft and airfield installations. In July 1944, just as the Japanese were being driven out of the Imphal plain, a daring raid under cover of darkness

*LAC Henry Kirk, an armourer in 2944 Field Squadron, with one of the mules used to take supplies to remote squadron positions in the hills around Imphal airfield in 1944.* (IWM-CI.684)

133

by a specialized Japanese infiltration group, Captain Inane's Butai, destroyed two Harvards, two Hurricanes and three Spitfires on the airfield at Palel. Some of the enemy were wounded by fire from a Regiment AA gun position and it was hoped that the follow-up airstrike might have caused further casualties among the Butai, but the redoubtable Captain Inane escaped, to reappear later elsewhere.

In May 1944 Group Captain B. A. Chacksfield, who was to become Commandant-General of the RAF Regiment as an air vice-marshal in 1963, but was then Org 1 at HQ ACSEA, issued instructions for the disbandment of all the AA flights by 31 July 1944 in order to release the manpower needed for the formation of LAA squadrons and additional field squadrons within the theatre. The resources provided by this measure enabled eight LAA squadrons and a further three field squadrons (numbered 2958 to 2968) to be formed at the Depot at Secunderabad between May and August 1944.

Later in 1944 the field squadrons were deployed to defend mobile radar units and the forward airfields from which the aircraft of 221 and 224 Groups were supporting XIVth Army's drive from India into Burma , with Rangoon as the ultimate objective. 2941 Squadron was in action at Imphal and Kangla before taking part in operations with 52 East African Brigade to prevent Japanese troops from escaping across the Chindwin River. Flights of 2943 Squadron operated up to 200 miles forward of their base at Palel with 14/13 Frontier Force Rifles, living on supplies dropped by air. Again from Palel, 2944 Squadron operated with 26 Brigade, taking part in the attack on Kalewa and becoming the first RAF unit to cross the Chindwin in September 1944.

Meanwhile, 2942, 2945 and 2946 Squadrons were deployed in the Arakan, operating in the area of Maungdaw, between the coast and the Mayu Hills. Towards the end of September, a flight of 2942 Squadron, commanded by Flight Lieutenant Angus Ian Mitchell, was attached to the 6th Oxfordshire & Buckinghamshire Light Infantry to assist in patrolling and locating enemy positions in the Mayu range which overlooked the coastal plain. In a company attack on a hill feature, the company commander was killed and the attack halted. Mitchell then took command and led a successful assault on the objective. In another patrol action a few days later the British force was surrounded by the enemy and was unable to break out. The patrol commander then ordered Mitchell to return to the company base and obtain artillery support to enable the patrol to withdraw to safety. While working his way through the encircling Japanese positions Flt Lt Mitchell was fired on by the enemy but he was able to reach the company base and report the situation, as a result of which the supporting fire plan enabled the

*Corporal Corcoran, LAC Shale, LAC Madrall and LAC Edgar preparing an RAF Regiment 20mm Hispano AA gun for action in Burma in 1945.* (IWM-CF.343)

patrol commander to extricate his men. For these actions he was awarded the Military Cross.

Despite the progress being made in the Mediterranean and North West-Europe, South-East Asia remained a "forgotten" theatre and as late as June 1944 the Air Ministry informed AHQ India that, due to the needs of 2TAF and the transfer of RAF Regiment personnel to the Army, there would be no reinforcement of the Regiment in South-East Asia. This caused consternation in 3TAF, for in May 1944 seven of the eight flying squadrons based on airfields in the Imphal plain had had to be withdrawn because there were insufficient Regiment forces available to defend their airfields. Air Marshal Sir John Baldwin, the AOC 3TAF, sent Group Captain Harris to London to put the ACSEA case for twelve field and eighteen LAA squadrons and he returned with an assurance that there would be no further reduction of the Regiment strength in the Far East and that priority would be given to finding appropriate Regiment reinforcements for ACSEA.

The dramatic change in the Air Ministry's perception of the situation which Jack Harris had achieved by his visit to London ensured that reinforcements began to arrive in India from October 1944 onwards. 1307 and 1308 Wing HQs, which had landed in Normandy on D+11, were both withdrawn from 2TAF and embarked for Bombay. Other wing HQs which were still in the UK, 1323, 1324, 1325, 1326, 1327, 1329, 1330 and 1331, also arrived in India before the end of 1944 and were deployed to exercise command of the increasing number of field and LAA squadrons in the theatre. However, as the RAF gained air

*Group Captain JH Harris OBE, Command Regiment Officer Air Command South East Asia, with Wing Commander Randle Manwaring and 2743 Field Squadron personnel on a forward airstrip in Burma in 1945.* (IWM-CF.566)

superiority in Burma the Japanese air force became a declining threat and many of the LAA squadrons were employed in the field role as the war progressed towards its end.

The arrival of 2706, 2837, 2852 and 2854 LAA Squadrons , together with 2708, 2739, 2743, 2748, 2759, 2802, 2810, 2846 and 2896 Field Squadrons, all from the UK, brought the Regiment order of battle in ACSEA up to ten wing HQs, sixteen field squadrons and twelve LAA squadrons in January 1945. The reinforcing units from the UK underwent arduous training courses at Argatala to accustom them to jungle operations and Squadron Leader Randle Manwaring, then OC 2743 Squadron, commented adversely on a training exercise which led to the death of one of his airmen. On the whole, however, the policy of "train hard, fight easy" paid dividends, as was proved by 1307 Wing at Meiktila only a few weeks later.

The availability of surplus armoured cars in the theatre made it possible to improve the flexibility of the Regiment by forming independent armoured car squadrons of the type which were already being used in Europe and the Mediterranean theatres, but without reducing the field squadrons to the establishment of rifle squadrons in other theatres. In February 1945 three armoured car squadrons (2970, 2971 and 2972) were formed at Secunderabad but only one, 2970, had been deployed operationally in Burma before the war ended.

By December 1944 the XIVth Army was across the Chindwin River and preparing for what the Japanese General Kimura termed "the battle of the Irrawaddy shore" as part of his plan for the defence of Mandalay. Kimura had concentrated the bulk of his forces to defend Mandalay in the belief that it was to be attacked by the whole of the British XIVth Army. This was, in fact, the result of an elaborate deception plan by General Slim to draw the Japanese armies to the north, while delivering the main attack by crossing the river further south and striking at Meiktila, the Japanese communications and administrative centre in

*LAC Gore, the leading scout of an RAF Regiment patrol, in Burma in 1945.*
(IWM-CF.568)

Burma. It was a brilliant example of the indirect approach and the result of the British plan was to enable XIVth Army to take Meiktila and drive south to capture Rangoon before the monsoon broke in May 1945.

At the end of February 1945 the 17th Indian Division struck at Meiktila and after hard fighting against a last-ditch Japanese defence the town was cleared and the airfield captured on 5 March. General Kimura thereupon ordered his 33rd Army south to recapture Meiktila and the rapid concentration of enemy units severed the British supply lines and isolated the British and Indian troops in Meiktila. The only solution to that was to both reinforce and resupply the garrison by air, for which use of the airfield at Meiktila East was now essential.

Wing Commander Michael Lander's 1307 Wing, consisting of 2708 Field Squadron supplemented by flights from 2941 and 2968 Field Squadrons and 2963 LAA Squadron, was flown in to Meiktila from Agartala on 6 March and placed under command of 99 Brigade. After taking up positions between Gurkha and Rajput companies within the defensive box overlooking the airfield, and digging their bunkers, the Regiment began patrolling the following day. It was necessary to sweep the

*Loading a 20mm Hispano of 2958 Squadron into a Dakota for a squadron redeployment by air – 1945* (Crown Copyright/MOD)

airfield every morning and to ensure that it was clear of the enemy before aircraft could begin flying in supplies and taking out casualties. At the end of each day all personnel and equipment had to be withdrawn into the box and preparations made for standing and fighting patrols to be sent out after nightfall. 2708 Squadron's 3″ mortar flight was absorbed into the brigade artillery line and carried out fire tasks in conjunction with Army field guns and medium mortars.

After several days and nights of constant patrol activity, Japanese artillery opened intensive fire on the box on 15 March. This closed the airfield and, during the barrage of 75mm and 105mm shells, a direct hit on a 2941 Squadron bunker caused several casualties. The enemy guns were eventually silenced by airstrikes and the airfield reopened for flying until darkness fell. Japanese infantry attacked the box during the night but were repulsed and, unknown to the defenders, took up positions on the airfield to await the morning sweep by 2708 Squadron. As two Regiment flights moved out of the box and into the open, two companies of enemy infantry opened fire from concealed positions on the airfield. Despite the strength of the opposition, the Regiment force pushed the Japanese back several hundred yards during a running fire fight. Flying Officer Furlong's flight was fortuitously reinforced by Flying Officer Kelly's flight, which was returning to base after mounting an overnight standing patrol beyond the airfield, but Flight Sergeant Norman Gerrish's flight was pinned down by enemy fire. Despite being wounded, Gerrish seized a Bren gun and gave covering fire to enable his men to withdraw and when he ran out of ammunition he picked up another Bren and continued firing to keep the enemy's heads down. When all his men had disengaged and reached safety, he walked calmly across open ground in full view of the enemy to rejoin his flight. The action had lasted for two hours, by which time a counter-attack force of tanks and two companies of infantry were assembled to reinforce the Regiment and the combined force cleared the enemy from the surrounds of the airfield. 2708 Squadron's casualties in this action were seven killed and eight wounded, but the Japanese left 150 of their dead and wounded behind. Surprisingly, Gerrish was not awarded the Distinguished Conduct Medal for which he had been strongly recommended, but received the lesser award of the Military Medal instead.

Michael Lander was tireless in commanding his wing and in setting a personal example to his officers and men. He insisted on leading from the front by participating in patrolling and in the daily sweeps of the airfield. It was while leading the morning sweep on 24 March that he and his runner, LAC Dakers, while ahead of the supporting flights, were both killed by enemy snipers. It was not until the Japanese were finally driven back from Meiktila that Flying Officer Kelly, Corporal McKenzie and LACs Bartlett, Finch and Hooson, were able to recover the bodies of Wing Commander Lander and LAC Dakers and give them temporary burial on the battlefield on 30th March. During the fighting 2708 Squadron had lost nine men killed in action, and 2963 Squadron a further four, in addition to many more wounded who were evacuated by air.

What was noteworthy about the Regiment's action at Meiktila was that the units involved had landed in India two months previously after a long sea voyage from the UK and had been sent directly into action only two days after completing their training at the forward echelon of the Depot at Agartala. The results reflected very favourably on the quality of the officers and airmen, some of whom were primarily anti-aircraft gunners, their training and combat skills, and the inspiring leadership of their Wing Commander.

The forward airfield at Ondauk was under constant threat from Japanese attack, which was kept at bay by the energetic patrol activity of 2945 Field Squadron until, in the early hours of 8 March 1945, the redoubtable Captain Inane and his Butai, disguised as Burmese peasants, reached the outskirts of the airfield. Surprised by a patrol from 2945 Squadron, led by Flight Lieutenant Hollingdale, a brief but intense fire fight followed and the intruders left an officer's pack and sword, radios, arms, ammunition and demolition charges on the bloodstained ground as they fled into the jungle taking their dead and wounded with them, among whom, it was hoped, might have been Captain Inane. One Japanese soldier was taken prisoner but when he attempted to escape he was shot and killed. Regiment casualties were one airman killed and three wounded.

*The graves of Wing Commader Lander and LAC W Dakers in the Commonwealth War Graves Cemetery at Htaukkyan, near Rangoon.* (ML Connolly)

In any event, this was the last attempt made by the enemy to infiltrate saboteurs onto an airfield. Sweeping south from Mandalay, the divisions of 33 Corps linked up with those of 4 Corps at Meiktila and continued to advance south on two axes, one along the Irrawaddy towards Mingaladon and Rangoon, the other along the Sittang to Toungoo and Rangoon. As a result, most of the Japanese 28th Army was trapped between the Irrawaddy, in the lower reaches of the Arakan, and the rugged mountains of the Pegu Yomas, from where the only escape to safety was towards the Japanese-held Shan hills to the east. The airfield at Toungoo was soon operational with two RAF fighter squadrons, and Squadron Leader Charles Killeen, wearing the hats of OC 2759 Field Squadron, acting OC 1307 Wing and Toungoo area defence commander, was responsible for blocking the enemy's escape routes to the north and south of the airfield. 2759 and 2964 Field, with 2963 and 2965 LAA Squadrons in the field

*Sergeant White, LAC Thompson, LAC Wingfield and LAC Priestley of 2759 Field Squadron in a captured Japanese bunker after the battle for Meiktila airfield.* (IWM-CI.1253)

role, mounted over eighty fighting patrols in appalling weather conditions and inflicted numerous casualties on the demoralized Japanese troops whose sole objective was to make their way to safety. At this point the GOC 19th Indian Division ordered 1307 Wing to send a fighting patrol to deal with a platoon of enemy troops who were reported to be in the area of Tabetgwe, some twenty miles west of Toungoo. Although 2759 Squadron was selected for this operation, most of the squadron's officers had been detached to support operations in the Arakan and the attack on Ramree Island, so the task of leading the patrol fell to a junior NCO.

Corporal Alex Miller, with Corporal Doverty as his deputy, and eighteen airmen from 2759 Squadron set off into the jungle for a ten-day patrol, mounted on fourteen elephants, ten of which each carried two airmen, with the remainder carrying ammunition, rations and supplies. It was the height of the monsoon season, the ground was waterlogged, the rivers and streams were overflowing and rain still fell steadily from the low dark clouds.

Establishing a patrol base at Shwekaung Ywathit, the patrol mounted attacks on two Japanese positions over the next two days, killing over twenty of the enemy, most of whom were sheltering from the weather in makeshift bashas, and seizing considerable quantities of arms and ammunition. Searches for enemy personnel who had been wounded, or escaped, revealed only dead bodies, the Japanese survivors having killed themselves with their own grenades rather than surrender. The sortie was successful in clearing a large area of the enemy, re-establishing a British presence among the local inhabitants and removing a potential threat to aircraft operating from Toungoo airfield. The patrol returned without loss, the only untoward incident occurring on the last night when one of the elephants was bitten by a snake and collapsed while fording a river. LACs Currie and Dixon were pitched into the fast-running water and had to make their own way back to the squadron base, ten miles away, on foot in the dark, leaving a dead elephant and its grieving mahout on the river bank.

The Regiment wings and squadrons had moved through Burma on two principal axes: one with 224 Group along the coast from Maungdaw to Akyab, Ramree Mingaladon and Rangoon; the other with 221 Group through central Burma from Ondauk to Mandalay, Meiktila, Toungoo and Pegu to Rangoon. Their primary task was to secure and defend the forward airfields from which the RAF provided air support to the Army; on over thirty occasions squadrons moved from one to the next by air, in other cases it took somewhat longer to move by road. General Slim, commander of XIVth Army, acknowledged that his Army's success was due to the superb support which it had received

*Operation "Dracula" - 2959 LAA Squadron marshalling 20mm Hispano guns after landing on the coast south of Rangoon in the monsoon rains of May 1945.* (IWM-CI.1368)

from the RAF, and, in his turn, Air Vice-Marshal Vincent, AOC 221 Group, made it clear that his ability to provide the best possible air support for the Army had depended on the reassuring levels of defence which his Regiment field and LAA squadrons provided for his airfields and forward radar installations, which were always sited far forward and close to the front line, and sometimes ahead of it. The value of the contribution made by the Regiment to air operations was subsequently confirmed by the AOC-in-C, Air Chief Marshal Sir Keith Park, in his final report on the campaign in South-East Asia.

The capture of Rangoon was planned on the basis of a pincer

*Wreckage of a Japanese BD17 shot down at Mingaladon by 2854 LAA Squadron – 1945.*
(Crown Copyright/MOD)

movement, with a land assault by 17th Division from the north and an amphibious landing (Operation *Dracula*) by 26th Division from the south. The Regiment's contribution to *Dracula* was 1327 Wing with 2959 LAA and 2967 Field Squadrons under command. Embarking at Akyab and Ramree, the landings were made at Elephant Point, fifteen miles south of Rangoon, in early May, just as the monsoon broke. By this time, the remaining troops of the Japanese 28th Army had taken refuge in the mountains of the Pegu Yomas and the area had to be cleared to remove any remaining threat to the re-establishment of civil administration throughout Burma. 1307 Wing, with five squadrons under command, was detached to General Tuker's 4 Corps which was tasked to deal with the break-out of the 18,000 enemy troops left in the Pegu Yomas. The main Japanese escape routes lay through 17th Division's area of responsibility, where 1307 Wing found itself operating alongside old friends from Meiktila and Toungoo days. The exhausted, and often starving, Japanese troops suffered over twelve thousand casualties in their attempts to escape; the total British losses were under a hundred killed and just over three hundred wounded.

Elsewhere action was in hand to restore the civil administration in the liberated areas of Burma and in April 1945 Wing Commander Graham Gow, who had variously commanded 1308, 1330 and 1331 Wings, was appointed to command a task force consisting of 2966 Field Squadron and detachments from 2706 and 2854 LAA Squadrons, drawn from 1326 Wing at Akyab, to escort Civil Affairs officers and medical support teams entering the Kaladan region of the Arakan. The expedition covered 2,600 square miles in little more than a month and was instrumental in restoring the pre-war structure of local government

*Wing Commander Graham Gow's task force, comprising officers and airmen of Nos. 2706 and 2854 LAA Squadrons, and 2966 Field Squadron, entering the Kaladan area of the Arakan by boat to re-establish British administration in the region in April 1945.* (IWM-CF.522)

*A 20mm Hispano AA gun position of 2962 LAA Squadron in the Cocos Islands in 1945.*
(IWM-CI.1501)

in that area. When the newly-appointed Governor of Burma arrived at Rangoon in October 1945, 2942 Field Squadron provided the guard of honour which received him.

Further afield, it had been decided to establish a transport and bomber airfield in the Cocos/Keeling Islands in the Indian Ocean, some 600 miles south-west of Java, to support projected operations against the Japanese in the former Dutch East Indies. 2962 LAA Squadron was detached to provide air defence during the construction of the airstrip and its subsequent operational use.

The next phase of the war in South East Asia was to be Operation *Zipper*, the invasion of Malaya (now Malaysia) and the recapture of Singapore, as a prelude to operations in Siam (now Thailand), Indo-China (now Vietnam) and the Dutch East Indies (now Indonesia). The RAF Regiment component of *Zipper* consisted of 2,500 officers and men in five Wing HQs with nine field squadrons and five LAA squadrons.

Tasked separately, after it was decided to rerole it as a parachute squadron, 2810 Field Squadron was assigned to Operation *Mastiff* as part of the Airborne Control Unit. This was intended to play an important part in controlling the air support for *Zipper* by parachuting small teams of aircrew, radio operators and Regiment gunners behind Japanese lines to identify targets for air attack in support of the landings. Squadron Leader (later Group Captain) Tony Sullivan was appointed to command 2810 Squadron and he interviewed and selected the volunteers for parachute training, among whom was Richard Auld, the

144

then Squadron Warrant Officer of 2759 Squadron at Toungoo. After completing the gruelling course at No.3 Parachute Training School at Chaklala, near Rawalpindi, Auld was posted to 2810 Parachute Squadron as its SWO. However, by then the war had ended and instead of parachuting into the Malayan jungle, 2810 Squadron reverted to being a field squadron and, in company with 2944 Squadron, sailed in October from Calcutta to Singapore where it was stationed at Kallang, the pre-war civil airport.

The abrupt ending of the war against Japan by the atomic bombs dropped on Hiroshima and Nagasaki in August 1945 produced an atmosphere of anti-climax in the British forces which were poised to invade Malaya and Singapore. The re-occupation of former British territories was delayed for a fortnight by the American insistence that nothing should be done to pre-empt the surrender ceremony on board American warships in Tokyo Bay. It was not until September, therefore, that *Zipper* could be belatedly put into effect. When the landing craft carrying 1324 Wing and 2748, 2846, 2852 and 2941 Squadrons moved towards the beaches at Morib, on the west coast of Malaya, they grounded some 600 yards from the shore and the squadrons had to wade

*Admiral Lord Louis Mountbatten, Supreme Commander South East Asia, speaking to LAC Cooper during his inspection of a Guard of Honour provided by 2942 Field Squadron (Squadron Leader AI Mitchell MC) at Rangoon in May 1945.* (IWM-CI.1403)

145

*Squadron Leader AI Mitchell MC leads 2942 Field Squadron to join the march-past in the Victory Parade at Rangoon.* (IWM-CI.1405)

ashore through three feet of water carrying supplies and equipment; had the landing been opposed, the results could have been disastrous for the assaulting troops. 2748 and 2846 Squadrons then drove to Singapore, becoming the first British units to travel that route, and to cross the Johore causeway, since 1942. 1324 Wing, with 2852 and 2941 Squadrons, moved to Kuala Lumpur and occupied the airfield there.

1329 Wing, with 2759, 2802, 2854, 2960 and 2965 Squadrons landed at Georgetown and took over the responsibility for Penang Island from the Royal Marines. The Wing enforced law and order, reinstated local government and even re-established the local radio station while enjoying the transition from the discomforts of the Burmese jungle to the luxurious surroundings of the Eastern & Oriental Hotel. 2759 Squadron acquired an unusual task when it was found that the inmates of a local leper colony were in a distressing state, having been half-starved and left without medical care during the Japanese occupation of the island. Arrangements were made for them to be taken to Kuala Lumpur for remedial treatment and Corporal Frederick Jeffrey

*Guard of Honour for Lieutenant-General Sir Frank Messervy, GOC 4 Corps, prior to his presentation of surrrendered Japanese swords to RAF Regiment squadrons.* (R Manwaring)

*2810 Field Squadron parading at the Cenotaph in Singapore on Remembrance Day in 1945. Note that parachute badges were worn above the right breast pocket in this unit.* (IWM-CI.1734)

and his section were given the task of escorting the special train which had been provided for the three-day journey. In due course the Wing Commander received an official letter of thanks, full of praise for the way in which Jeffrey and his men had carried out this difficult task, from the authorities in Kuala Lumpur.

1331 Wing, with 2706, 2708 and 2743 Squadrons landed in Hong Kong and occupied Kai Tak airfield while 1307 Wing with 2963 and 2967 Squadrons took over Tan Son Nhut airfield at Saigon and 2945 Squadron was airlifted to Bangkok to defend the RAF aircraft based at Dom Muang airport. 2810, 2896, 2944 and 2964 Squadrons had been deployed to Singapore where they occupied the airfields of Kallang, Tengah, Seletar and the Japanese-built airfield at Changi as well as moving into Tanglin barracks with the Army. 2896 Squadron mounted a guard of honour for Admiral Lord Mountbatten who was sufficiently impressed to invite the squadron commander to send a representative to the forthcoming surrender ceremony in the centre of Singapore. Picked as the smartest man on parade, Corporal William Vance was nominated to attend and witness the Japanese generals sign the instrument of surrender. In March 1946 2964 Squadron sent a representative flight to Japan as part of the British occupation forces.

Although the immediate post-war chaos in Singapore and Malaya soon returned to a semblance of the pre-war situation, it took some time to restore an efficient administration in Hong Kong, which had been occupied by Chinese troops by the time the British returned. There were several instances of friction between the Regiment squadrons which were employed on security duties at the harbour, in support of the civil police, and Chinese soldiers who may have believed that they had a prior right to the colony. Fortunately, the Chinese Army was soon withdrawn from the Colony and normality began to return to Hong

*2896 Field Squadron disembarking at Singapore docks, September 1945.* (R Manwaring)

Kong. 2708 Squadron provided the escort on board a ship returning 3,000 Japanese prisoners of war to Japan in December 1945 and 2706 Squadron's last task was to provide the guard of honour for the arrival of the new governor of Hong Kong shortly before the squadron was disbanded in May 1946.

In Thailand the RAF presence at Dom Muang was not perceived as a threat to Thai independence and there was no apparent hostility towards British personnel. There were, however, constant incursions onto the airfield by locals who were looking for desirable items which would fetch a price on the black market. Regiment airmen were kept fully occupied in protecting the RAF enclave, with its aircraft, equipment and fuel stocks and their success in doing so inevitably generated frustration and aggression among those Thais who resented this obstacle to their entrepreneurial activities. In February 1946 a 2945 Squadron patrol intercepted a group of infiltrators at night and in the ensuing mêlée and pursuit one of the airmen in the patrol became separated from his comrades and was surrounded and killed by the intruders who took his rifle and ammunition and threw his body into a lake.

In French Indo-China the various nationalist groups were determined to establish their own rule before the French could return and the arrival of British forces to disarm the Japanese garrisons provoked a confrontation with Annamite and Vietminh forces. The first RAF aircraft to arrive at Tan Son Nhut received a hostile reception from the local Annamite commander and an urgent call for RAF Regiment support resulted in Wing Commander Allen, with HQ 1307 Wing and

148

2963 LAA Squadron, arriving by air at Saigon airport on 1 October 1945. The airfield, which contained numerous fuel and ammunition dumps as well as aircraft, was far too large an area for a single squadron to defend and 2967 Field Squadron was embarked at Rangoon to reinforce 1307 Wing by sea. In addition, Wing Commander Allen co-opted the resident Japanese infantry battalion into 1307 Wing to assist in the defence of the airfield. The battalion operated enthusiastically under its commander, Major Matsuzato, and his officers alongside the two Regiment squadrons in countering infiltration and attacks by Vietnamese rebel forces. In spite of this, Squadron Leader Ward of 2963 Squadron was shot and wounded when the vehicle in which he was travelling to Saigon was ambushed and the number of hostile incidents increased until, in February 1946, the French Air Force took over responsibility for the airfield and the RAF Regiment was able to withdraw from Indo-China.

At that stage Major Matsuzato surrendered his sword to the senior RAF Regiment officer in Saigon and he and his men were shipped back to Japan. When 1307 Wing HQ was disbanded in March 1946, there were still four airmen on its strength who had served continuously with the HQ from its formation at Westhampnett in May 1944 through Normandy, France and the Low Countries to India, Burma (including Meiktila) and Indo-China.

Meanwhile, in the Dutch East Indies the internal situation was going from bad to worse as all British personnel, whether Service or civilian, were treated as enemies by Indonesian nationalists who believed that they were supporting the restoration of Dutch colonial rule. This situation was exploited, and encouraged, by some Japanese officers who evaded surrender and incited the Indonesian nationalist leadership to engage in armed insurrection, using Japanese arms and ammunition,

*Personnel of 2854 LAA Squadron landing at Labuan – 1945.* (Crown Copyright/MOD)

against Allied personnel when they arrived to take the surrender of the Japanese military and to rescue some 70,000 Allied prisoners of war and civilian internees in Java and Sumatra. Accordingly, the first British teams, which arrived in Java as part of a revamped Operation *Mastiff* to evacuate the captives, were treated with open hostility by fanatical and well-armed Indonesian rebels. The abduction and murder of some members of these British teams by Indonesians, who had been urged by renegade Japanese officers to regard all Europeans as their enemies, forced the deployment of British Army and RAF units to Java and Sumatra to enable the prisoners of war and internees to be rescued, sometimes from Indonesian mobs intent on holding them as hostages, or even of killing them in cold blood. In November 1945 an RAF Dakota crashed near Bekassi, only seven miles from Batavia, but by the time a patrol from 2962 Squadron reached the wrecked aircraft, the civilian passengers, who included women and children, and the crew who had survived the crash had been abducted and murdered by Indonesian rebels and their mutilated bodies scattered in the undergrowth.

Parachutists from 2810 Field Squadron formed part of the *Mastiff* teams which were dropped into Java and Sumatra in September 1945 and in an action at Surabaya when one team was attacked, and suffered casualties, Corporal Lionel Groome, a medical orderly in 2810 Squadron, not only tended the wounded but left his medical pack to pick up a light machine gun, which he used to good effect in repelling the attackers. Groome was subsequently awarded the Military Medal.

1308 Wing with 2943 and 2962 Squadrons, the latter squadron fresh from its deployment to the Cocos Islands under command, were deployed to the airfield of Kemajoran, outside the town of Batavia in Java in October 1945 to protect the RAF aircraft which were operating from there. When five British officers (including Squadron Leader Tanfield, OC 2943 Squadron) flew to Surabaya for a meeting with Indonesian authorities there, they were arrested, imprisoned, ill-treated, and stripped of their possessions before being eventually released. During their time in an Indonesian prison the only help which they received was from some Japanese officers who were also confined there, albeit under rather better conditions than the British officers were held.

In November, 2962 Squadron provided the escort for the burial of a British airman at the civilian cemetery in Batavia. During the funeral ceremony Indonesian forces opened fire on the mourners but the NCO in charge of the Regiment detachment, Sergeant Alec Haines, deployed his men to return the fire and covered the withdrawal of the others attending the funeral. When all had safely returned to the vehicles,

Haines took a party back to the cemetery to recover the coffin and then led the convoy back to the airfield, despite further attacks being made in attempts to halt the vehicles. For his initiative and disregard of his own safety under fire, Alec Haines was awarded the Military Medal.

By December 1945 the British forces had completed their humanitarian mission in Java and were preparing to leave the island. The RAF had withdrawn from the airfield at Kemajoran and 1308 Wing and 2943 Squadron had concentrated, with the Army, at Tanah Tinggi barracks in Batavia. The final episode in this necessary, but distasteful, operation was an assault on the RAF Regiment sector of the barracks by a large Indonesian force, which was defeated and driven off after heavy losses had been inflicted on the attackers by 2943 Squadron.

In Sumatra the focal point of the rescue operation was at Medan and 1323 Wing was deployed there in October 1945, with 2837, 2961 and 2968 Squadrons, to secure the airfield which was being used by RAF aircraft. The involvement of British forces in Sumatra lasted longer than it did in Java and in January 1946 2739 Squadron had to be sent from India to replace 1323 Wing and its squadrons, all of which had become non-operational by the repatriation of most of their officers and airmen to the UK.

In June 1946 a section of 2739 Squadron was defending a radio installation outside the airfield perimeter when it was attacked, under cover of darkness, by an Indonesian rebel group, some forty strong, armed with a variety of weapons. The section commander, LAC Holbrook, immediately responded by leading his section of six airmen against the more numerous attackers and in the ensuing fighting Holbrook and LAC Parker were hacked to death and two others seriously injured while the remaining three members of the section were also wounded. When the alarm was raised, the squadron commander, Squadron Leader Williams, led the reserve flight in a counter-attack which killed a number of the Indonesian attackers and restored the situation. As the only RAF Regiment unit in Sumatra, 2739 Squadron also became seriously under strength due to the repatriation of its time-expired personnel and reinforcements of an officer and seventy-five NCOs and airmen had to be sent to Medan from the equally under-strength 2941 Squadron in Kuala Lumpur.

In June 1946 reports were received that a number of former civilian internees were still being held hostage at an Indonesian rebel camp in the jungle near the town of Padang in Sumatra. George Lawrence was a member of the flight of 2810 Field Squadron which was flown from Singapore to reinforce troops of the Royal Garwhal Rifles and the Punjab Regiment for a rescue operation. The combined force left

*2943 Field Squadron roadblock near Kemajoran, Java – 1945.* (Crown Copyright/MOD)

Padang just before midnight and after a cautious approach march attacked the Indonesian camp at first light. Complete surprise was achieved and fifty-two hostages were released and ten armed Indonesians taken prisoner. On the way back to the airstrip at Padang the relief party was ambushed by another Indonesian group, of whom seventeen were killed and three captured in the ensuing skirmish, with the loss of two Indian soldiers killed and one wounded. The 2810 Squadron detachment remained in Sumatra and a few weeks later carried out another attack on an Indonesian jungle base, killing nineteen Indonesians and capturing five, without loss to themselves. Returning from Padang to Medan, and taking with them several surrendered Japanese soldiers, the 2810 Squadron detachment embarked for the return journey to Singapore by sea at the end of July. The last Regiment personnel left Sumatra in August 1946.

It is of interest to note that there were more British casualties sustained in the Dutch East Indies from 1945 to 1946 than anywhere else in that post-war period. The official RAF history records that "the vigilance and courage of the RAF Regiment gunners throughout this difficult period was beyond praise, and they suffered a number of casualties as a result of enemy action."

Elsewhere in the Far East there were problems of another sort. Repatriation to the United Kingdom was slow, partly because of a lack of shipping and partly because the British government, uncertain about

152

*Major-General AE Robinson DSO, Commandant RAF Regiment, speaking to LAC Ashley during his inspection of 2810 Field Squadron at Kallang airfield in Singapore in 1946. He is accompanied by the squadron commander, Squadron Leader H Sullivan.* (IWM-CF.857)

the political situation in the liberated colonial territories, wished to retain a substantial military force east of Suez in order to maintain stability in a potentially volatile area. While the soldiers were generally fully employed in various military roles, the reduction in the RAF's flying effort resulted in the majority of airmen in the technical and administrative trades becoming bored and dissatisfied with their lot. It was fertile ground for agitators with various motives and in 1946 a series of "strikes" against authority, a veiled form of mutiny, started on large RAF stations in India and spread through the Far East. It is worth remembering that no RAF Regiment unit took any part in this action and even on stations where most of the other airmen participated in demonstrations, Regiment airmen continued to work normally and ignored the protestors and the blandishments of the agitators. The close relationship of officers, NCOs and airmen within Regiment squadrons maintained discipline and esprit-de-corps, setting a positive example to those often leaderless RAF tradesmen who were often confused as to which side of the fence they should be.

Of the ten wing headquarters and thirty-three squadrons of the RAF Regiment in ACSEA on VJ-Day 1945 all but one had been disbanded by the end of 1946. The sole survivor was 2810 Squadron, which remained in Singapore until it was replaced by the formation of the RAF Regiment (Malaya) in 1947.

# THE SOUTH-EAST ASIA CAMPAIGN IN RETROSPECT

This campaign, which was principally fought in Burma, shared some characteristics with the one in the Middle East, where both Commands were concerned with forming and training RAF Regiment units while engaged in active operations against a formidable enemy. There were, both in Egypt and India, well-established peacetime headquarters which were capable of rapid expansion to meet the demands of war and in both cases RAF Regiment staff structures fitted easily alongside the other RAF staff divisions. Although the headquarters of ACSEA was in Ceylon, some distance from the combat zone in Burma, the organization of the Air Force into seven groups enabled Regiment staff officers to be established at the Group HQs to direct ground defence planning and to monitor the deployment and operations of Regiment wings and squadrons in the field.

The Command Defence Officer, Group Captain Jack Harris, was, above all, an outstanding staff officer who planned, managed, controlled and integrated the RAF Regiment operations throughout ACSEA in detail. He achieved excellent working relationships with the senior commanders and their staffs, and successfully obtained support from the Air Ministry in reinforcing ACSEA with Regiment units at a critical time. His strengths were as a talented and able staff officer, rather than as a commander, but his skill ensured the support and resources which his units needed to achieve their undoubted success in the long and hard campaign which finally destroyed the Japanese army and air force in Burma.

The similarities in the staff structures in ACSEA, MEAF and 2TAF were worthy of note, in each of these theatres competent headquarters staffs managed the deployment of Regiment units to ensure the maximum effectiveness of the RAF's resources for integrated ground and air operations. The other notable feature of the campaign in Burma was the frequent movement of Regiment squadrons, including their weapons and equipment, by air to ensure their rapid deployment to forward airfields and radar installations. Their success was reflected in Air Chief Marshal Sir Keith Park's final report on RAF operations in ACSEA, in which he praised the invaluable contribution which the Regiment squadrons had made to the success of the air war. Nevertheless, when the opportunity arose for the Regiment to provide assistance to hard-pressed Army formations by committing squadrons to carry out infantry or reconnaissance tasks, this was done without prejudicing the RAF's requirements, which always received priority. The pattern for the Regiment's long-term roles within the Royal Air Force was tested, and confirmed, in the operations of Air Command South-East Asia.

154

*'Lofty' and 'Titch' haggling in a market in Java – 1945.* (Crown Copyright/MOD)

## WING HEADQUARTERS IN ACSEA 1944-1946

**1307** – From UK to Bombay December 1944 – Ondauk – Meiktila – Toungoo – Pegu – Saigon. Disbanded March 1946.

**1308** – From UK to Bombay December 1944 – Chittagong – Maungdaw – Java – Batavia – Tanah Tinggi. Disbanded May 1946.

**1323** – Formed Secunderabad July 1944 – Palel – Imphal – Magwe – Sumatra – Medan. Disbanded April 1946.

**1324** – Formed Secunderabad July 1944 – Tullihal – Shwebo – Morib – Singapore. Disbanded February 1946.

**1325** – Formed Secunderabad October 1944 – Disbanded February 1946.

**1326** – Formed Secunderabad October 1944 – Maungdaw – Akyab – Insein – Penang – Singapore. Disbanded May 46.

**1327** – Formed Secunderabad October 1944 – Chittagong – Ramree – Mingaladon – Singapore – Kuala Lumpur. Disbanded January 1946.

**1329** – From UK to Bombay December 1944 – Agartala – Monywa – Mingaladon – Penang – Singapore. Disbanded February 1946.

**1330** – From UK to Bombay January 1945 – Agartala – Toungoo – Pegu – Rangoon. Disbanded March 1946.

**1331** – From UK to Bombay January 1945 – Agartala – Chittagong – Akyab – Hong Kong. Disbanded May 46. Awards: 1 MID

## SQUADRONS IN ACSEA 1943 – 1946

**2706 LAA** From UK to Bombay December 1944 – Agartala – Dohazari – Maungdaw – Akyab – Hong Kong. Disbanded May 46.

**2708 Field** From UK to Bombay January 1945 – Agartala – Meiktila – Toungoo – Calcutta – Hong Kong. Awards: 1 MM+1 MID Disbanded May 1946.

**2739 Field** From UK to Bombay November 1944 – Secunderabad – Calcutta –   Chittagong – Maungdaw – Warangal – Madras – Sumatra – Medan. Awards: 3 MID. Disbanded August 1946.

**2743 Field** From UK to Bombay January 1945 – Agartala – Ondauk – Ondaw – Calcutta – Hong Kong. Disbanded February 1946.

**2748 Field** From UK to Bombay January 1945 – Agartala – Santa Cruz – Malaya – Singapore – Tengah – Java – Batavia – Surabaya – Bali. Disbanded April 1946.

**2759 Field** From UK to Bombay October 1944 – Secunderabad – Chittagong – Chiringa – Meiktila – Toungoo – Penang – Singapore – Tengah. Disbanded April 1946.

**2802 Field** From UK to Bombay January 1945 – Agartala – Dwhala – Kalawya – Rangoon – Penang – Kuala Lumpur. Awards: 1 BEM. Disbanded February 1946.

**2810 Field** From UK to Bombay January 1945 – Agartala – Chaklala – Parachute trained – Calcutta – Singapore – Op *Mastiff* – Java – Sumatra. Awards: 1 MM

**2837 LAA** From UK to Bombay October 1944 – Calcutta – Chittagong – Ramu – Cox's Bazar – Ramree – Madras – Singapore – Sumatra – Medan. Disbanded April 1946.

**2846 Field** From UK to Bombay January 1945 – Secunderabad – Santa Cruz – Malaya – Singapore – Seletar. Disbanded March 1946.

**2852 LAA** From UK to Bombay January 1945 – Secunderabad – Santa Cruz – Malaya – Kuala Lumpur. Disbanded March 1946.

**2854 LAA** From UK to Bombay October 1944 – Secunderabad – Akyab – Sinthe – Magwe – Mingaladon – Rangoon – Penang – Borneo – Labuan. Disbanded April 1946.

**2896 Field** From UK to Bombay January 1945 – Agartala – Chittagong – Madras – Singapore. Awards: 1 MID. Disbanded June 1946.

**2941 Field** Formed Secunderabad April 1943 – Imphal – Kangla – Ondauk – Meiktila – Mingaladon – Malaya – Kuala Lumpur. Disbanded July 1946.

**2942 Field** Formed Secunderabad May 1943 – Comilla – Maungdaw – Chittagong – Rangoon – Mingaladon. Awards: 1 OBE+1 MC+1 MID. Disbanded June 1946.

**2943 Field** Formed Secunderabad May 1943 – Jessore – Palel – Saudang – Toungoo – Madras – Java – Batavia – Kemajoran. Disbanded March 1946.

**2944 Field** Formed Secunderabad June 1943 – Chittagong – Imphal – Palel – Yalagyo – Taukkyan – Sinthe – Magwe – Meiktila – Singapore – Tanglin. Awards: 1 MID. Disbanded January 1946.

**2945 Field** Formed Secunderabad June 1943 – St Paul's Island – Maungdaw – Ondauk – Ondaw – Rangoon – Bangkok – Dom Muang. 1 MID. Disbanded June 1946.

**2946 Field** Formed Secunderabad July 1943 – Chittagong – Maungdaw – Tullihal – Sinthe. Disbanded January 1946.

**2958 LAA** Formed Secunderabad May 1944 – Chittagong – Palel – Tamu – Kalemyo – Sinthe – Magwe – Rangoon – Warangal. Disbanded January 1946.

**2959 LAA** Formed Secunderabad June 1944 – Agartala – Cox's Bazar – Patenga – Ramree – Rangoon – Mingaladon – Warangal. Disbanded January 1946.

**2960 LAA** Formed Secunderabad June 1944 – Imphal – Ondauk – Ondaw – Dwhela – Rangoon – Penang. Awards: 1 MID. Disbanded May 1946.

**2961 LAA**  Formed Secunderabad July 1944 – Dimapur – Tullihal – Palel – Tabingaung – Saudang – Rangoon – Sumatra – Medan. Disbanded January 1946.

**2962 LAA**  Formed Secunderabad July 1944 – Cocos Islands – Colombo – Madras – Java – Batavia – Kemajoran. Awards: 1 MM+1 MID. Disbanded August 1946.

**2963 LAA**  Formed Secunderabad August 1944 – Cox's Bazar – Ramree – Imphal –Yalagyo – Meiktila – Toungoo – Hmwabi – Saigon. Disbanded March 1946.

**2964 LAA**  Formed Secunderabad August 1944 – Dimapur – Alipore – Toungoo – Rangoon – Penang – Singapore. Disbanded March 1946.

**2965 LAA**  Formed Secunderabad August 1944—Imphal – Meiktila – Toungoo – Rangoon – Penang – Butterworth – Singapore – Tanglin. Disbanded March 1946.

**2966 Field**  Formed Secunderabad August 1944 – Comilla – Dohazari – Akyab – Madras – Singapore – Seletar. Disbanded July 1946.

**2967 Field**  Formed Secunderabad September 1944 – Dohazari – Chiringa – Ramree – Rangoon – Saigon. Disbanded February 1946.

**2968 Field**  Formed Secunderabad September 1944 – Tullihal – Imphal – Mutaik – Ondauk – Meiktila – Mingaladon – Rangoon – Sumatra – Medan. Disbanded January 1946.

**2970 Armoured Car**  Formed Secunderabad February 1945 – Agartala – Rangoon – Mingaladon. Disbanded April 1946.

**2971 Armoured Car**  Formed Secunderabad February 1945 – Disbanded March 1946.

**2972 Armoured Car**  Formed Secunderabad February 1945 – Disbanded March 1946.

# EPILOGUE

It was no mean achievement for the Royal Air Force to have created a specialized ground fighting force from scratch in the early stages of a major war and one which, in three and a half years of war, had supported air operations in every theatre of war, as well as carrying out a multiplicity of additional tasks, including being in action alongside the Army, on a worldwide basis. By 1945 the RAF Regiment had broken new ground by ensuring that the Royal Air Force did not have to rely on another Service for the defence of its airfields and installations against ground and air attack, thus giving the RAF a freedom of action in the exercise of air power which it had not enjoyed before 1942.

Growing up under the constraints and pressures of war inevitably resulted in some mistakes and wasted effort, but it also accelerated the learning curve for everyone in the new force. By the end of the war in Europe and the Far East, during which time a total of thirty-nine wing headquarters and 266 LAA, field, rifle and armoured car squadrons had been formed to meet changing operational needs, the RAF had a competent and battle-hardened ground fighting force at its disposal. In common with the remainder of the RAF, the Regiment was run down as rapidly as possible once the war ended but, unlike those in the pre-war established RAF branches and trades, there was no long-term plan for the retention of RAF Regiment officers and airmen because the place of the Regiment in the peace-time establishment of the Air Force was not resolved until 1947. Inevitably, many of those who would have volunteered to continue serving in the Regiment, had its future been clear, left to seek careers elsewhere and many able officers, NCOs and aircraftmen were lost to the post-war Regiment in this period of indecision.

Sadly, the indiscriminate disbanding of squadrons, without any thought of retaining the identities of those with distinguished combat records, also resulted in the irretrievable loss of any future claim for many of the battle honours which had been earned in actions in North Africa, the Mediterranean, the Far East and North-West Europe. Those campaigns and battles could have been borne proudly on the Standards of the Regiment squadrons which exist today, had any thought been given to preserving the heritage of the war-time squadrons for the post-war years.

Major-General Sir Claude Liardet, the Territorial Royal Artillery officer who had so brilliantly directed the RAF Regiment's organization

*Victory Parade, London 1946.* (R. Rollit)

and deployments throughout the testing years of war, returned to civilian life shortly after VE Day and the Air Ministry turned to the War Office for his successor. Major-General A. E. Robinson, a regular infantry officer, late of the Green Howards, was appointed to the post which he held until 1948. From then onwards, conscious of the need to demonstrate that the Regiment was an integral part of the Royal Air Force, the Air Ministry ensured that subsequent Commandant Generals were appointed from within the Royal Air Force.

After conflicting views about the post-war composition of the Royal Air Force had been reconciled within the Air Council, the RAF Regiment was recognized as a permanent part of the RAF in 1947, with an established strength of 3,300 all ranks in a peacetime Air Force numbering 200,000 officers and airmen. By 1952 this had risen to just under eight thousand officers and men in eighteen wing headquarters and forty-seven squadrons, with a further twenty-one squadrons of the RAF Levies (Iraq), the Aden Protectorate Levies and the RAF

*Air Vice-Marshal J H Harris CB CBE Commandant-General RAF Regiment 1959-1961. He was the first RAF Regiment officer to be appointed to this position.* (RAF Regiment Museum)

*Major-General Sir Claude Liardet KBE CB DSO (1881-1966) Commandant RAF Regiment 1942-1945.* (RAF Regiment Museum)

Regiment (Malaya) in the Middle East and the Far East.

From then onwards the size of the RAF Regiment fluctuated, its peaks and troughs reflecting the changing roles, strengths and deployments of the Royal Air Force, which, of course, it exists to serve. In difficult times, when the defence of the realm was under political and economic pressures, the Regiment demonstrated its flexibility and adaptability in taking on new tasks within the Air Force while maintaining the high professional standards which enhanced its credibility within the wider Defence establishment, including other air forces. In working alongside its NATO allies, the example set by the

RAF Regiment has caused several of them to revise their own organization for airfield defence along the lines successfully demonstrated by the Royal Air Force.

Sixty years after its formation in the crucible of war, the RAF Regiment continues to make its unique contribution towards the operational capabilities of the Royal Air Force. Readily accepting a wider range of roles in order to add to the effectiveness of air power wherever the RAF operates, the RAF Regiment continues to maintain its roles as both a Corps in its own right and an integral part of the Royal Air Force. That it is able to do so is in no small measure due to the examples set, and the sacrifices made, by the officers and airmen of the embryonic RAF Regiment in the formative and testing war-time years of 1942 to 1946.

**PER ARDUA**

# INDEX